FIRST EDITION

TARRED AND FEATHERED... AGAIN
THE ONGOING IMPACT OF THE RACIAL ATTACKS ON PRESIDENT OBAMA

By Darwin B. Fishman, Ph.D.

cognella® | ACADEMIC PUBLISHING

Bassim Hamadeh, CEO and Publisher

Angela Schultz, Acquisitions Editor

Michelle Piehl, Project Editor

Berenice Quirino, Associate Production Editor

Miguel Macias, Senior Graphic Designer

Trey Soto, Licensing Associate

Don Kesner, Interior Designer

Natalie Piccotti, Senior Marketing Manager

Kassie Graves, Director of Acquisitions and Sales

Jamie Giganti, Senior Managing Editor

Cover image copyright © 2014 iStockphoto LP/mashuk.

Printed in the United States of America.

ISBN: 978-1-5165-2906-3 (pbk) / 978-1-5165-2907-0 (br)

DEDICATION

To those that have passed on in my circle: my uncle, Fred Perry, my aunt, Helene Goodwin, and my mom, Sylvia Fishman.

To my current Other Mothers: Jo Ann Livoni, Dr. Essie Rutledge, and my cousin, Anne Hurst, and to my father, Jerry Fishman, AKA Big Daddy Fish.

Much respect and love for the elders that always tried to extend love and wisdom to me during the most benign and treacherous time.

ACKNOWLEDGEMENTS

While I couldn't have foreseen the obstacles I would encounter along the path to creating this book, I am grateful for the ongoing assistance of my editor, Michelle Piehl, and the counsel of Kassie Graves, director of acquisitions and sales. I want to really thank my father, Jerry Fishman, for all the labors of love he did for this book from reviewing and commenting

CONTENTS

on the initials drafts to the cover art at the end of this process. I also want to thank my brother, Wendell Fishman, and I want to say to him, "Yes, we will always be family." Even after all we've been through and what we continue to encounter, the three Fish Men will move on bounded by destiny and blood. There have been many folks that have supported and nurtured this book project that I could not begin to name all of them, but I do want it known their kindness and care did help and did make it possible for me to reach this endpoint. Let me give a final shout out to Buki and her boys—they have not only filled my life with much joy, but they have also shown me how six together can overcome the most formidable life obstacles.

INTRODUCTION

OBAMA'S PRESIDENCY AND THE RACIAL ASSAULT

In one important respect, however, McCain's run for president differed notably from those of the elder Bush and of Dole. His campaign rates as one of the least negative waged by Republicans presidential candidates since 1960. Moreover, Obama's campaign ranks dead last in Democrat negativity. Overall, 2008 shows up as the least negative of thirteen presidential contests in forty-eight years.

Buell, Jr., and Sigelman, 2008

INTRODUCTION

What I have been most struck by since Barack Obama was elected as our 44th president in 2008 has been how unremarkable and arguably very

1

predictable this "new" venture has been for large portions of our country. The election of the first African American President did not result in mass race riots, an impeachment trial, or reparations for African Americans, or even an assassination of a president. In fact, from the vantage point of those most oppressed in our society, one could argue not a great deal changed, and in that sense Obama was not too different from any other modern era President—Democrat and Republican administrations included. Part of the paradox built in and around the Obama presidency is the fact that extraordinary policy initiatives and bold executive Office actions distinguished the Obama presidency from almost every other former president. Based on the biting critiques of the president from the right and the left of the political spectrum, one would never guess that the status quo was kept relatively intact despite the seismic progressive shifts in policy presided over by President Obama. In spite of the rhetoric most closely associated with right-wing, conservative criticisms, one could easily refute the charges that the U.S. became more socialist, less secure, or even radically increased the national debt. The same holds true for some critiques of the left about military adventures, eroding of civil liberties, or economic security. Placed in the context of previous Democratic and Republican Presidents, very little about the Obama administration's governing style, policy development, and advocacy stands out as ground-breaking or as politically radically. Even in Obama's most successful policy initiative achievements, such as the Affordable Health Care Act, the actual policy debate and national discourse did not deviate significantly from the Clinton administration's attempt to pass national health care initiatives. Given this background, why were there such intense and hyper-polarization of political divides during the Obama presidency?

To answer this question, I not only examined the central distinguishing feature of the Obama presidency (racial identity), but I also examined the way that this feature of the presidency elicited a public response (racial reaction). Specifically, the way in which Obama's racial identity was openly and negatively challenged through racial images and messages has become the most significant foundational component of his presidency. A case will be made for how an African American president is not only historically unique, but the racial assault Obama experienced had a tremendous impact on his political campaigns, as well as his governing style and the development of his legislative agenda (Chapters II and VI).

One way this phenomenon can be examined is through the way in which a mythic Obama was constructed by his followers as well as his detractors. This mythic-Obama making included the inadvertent or purposeful neglect of the racial assaults that were directed at this presidency in a way that has never historically occurred. The tension this can create for those attempting to assess the Obama administration has been pronounced not just from the standpoint of those who had such high expectations for the first Black President, but also from those who most wanted to see Obama's presidency as a complete failure. From the side of those who had high expectations, it became clear that many of these lofty goals and principles ultimately ran into the reality of what anyone in charge of the executive branch might be able to accomplish at this point in history. A key component of this critique hinged upon Obama's racial identity and exactly how "Black" he was. Put simply, if he was really "Black," then he would not "sell out," and he would really deliver the goods to all of the downtrodden masses. The racial logic follows the opening provided by Obama's biracial identity, which allowed some to question his racial allegiance and the authenticity of his Black experience. One of the most striking aspects of this situation was the lack of appreciation and understanding of how little could and would change with an Obama presidency. This is not to suggest that the president and the executive branch has insignificant or does not possess significant power, nor is this an attempt to claim that even though this power has been used in very limited and narrowly defined ways, that questions about who the president is and what a president accomplishes are not worthy of analysis and debate. It is important to note that historically the power wielded by presidents has been rarely used to help those truly at the margins in society, and to the extent this power was utilized for these groups, it provided, at best, mixed results (Walters, 2003). Given this reality, coupled with the added element of the United States experiencing the worst economic recession in 2008 and 2009 since the 1930s, it is worth thinking about what any president could have accomplished since 2008, especially a moderate African American male Democrat. In particular, with the added attention and enthusiasm attached to the election of the first African American president, it was presumed that those most disadvantaged in society would have an ally, or at least someone more sympathetic to their plight. This leads to questions such as, "How did this expectation translate into real-life governing style and policy development?" "Was this a realistic expectation of Obama or any president?" "Are there tangible differences between what White and Non-White occupants of the White House can accomplish?" "What impact did race and racism have on the first African American president?" being asked and addressed from the standpoint of what Obama accomplished and neglected during his two terms as president.

What I discovered is that the critiques of the Obama administration, whether ideological in nature or not, plowed some very familiar ground, but also remarkably left some fertile terrain untouched for developing analysis of the Obama administration. This was not only true for critiques most typically associated with the right end of the political spectrum, but this neglect of central features of the Obama administration was also missed by critics associated with the left. It was not the case that the unprecedented intense political assault from the right immobilized the Obama administration, and these attacks were able to stymie every aspect of Obama's political agenda. Some areas of policy and diplomatic success that Obama experienced, especially within his first term, could arguably be compared favorably to any other modern-era President. It was the way Obama had to navigate through and address the potential for racial backlash and address fully visible racial assaults that left the most inedible mark on his presidency. I was able to identify and track elements of racist attacks that were launched by political opponents, and I was able to establish how effective they were, not just as way to incapacitate the Obama administration, but the way in which they contorted and distorted Obama's political campaigns and his administration. In particular, the racist attacks leveled at Obama became a unique feature of how Obama conducted his political campaigns and how he developed his policy agenda and governing style. These attacks could be considered so potent that a case could be made that they had an overt impact not just on his campaigns and governing style, but they had a profound connection to anything that might be construed as supporting racial minorities and those most marginalized in our society. The most intriguing point I discovered in my work was not how executive branch power looks and feels from the vantage point of racial minorities, but how tenacious the terrain was for the first African American president to wade through to address racial inequality and misery in even a limited liberal Democratic Party traditional fashion.

What I began to explore were the limits any president might encounter if he/she attempted to address the concerns the vast majority of racial minorities encounter on a daily basis, coupled with the fact that Obama's status as the first Black president might complicate or simplify an analysis of these traditional limits. While studying this topic, I began to appreciate how much the election process could not only set the tone for a presidency but could also literally lock a president into a particular governing style and public policy agenda. This is exactly what I uncovered when examining the 2008 presidential elections from the perspective of traditional social science research and from the vantage point of scholars who work on identity, White Nationalism, and racism. Obama has not only encountered and struggled with an executive branch mired in a racist structure, but, by virtue of his identity, he started his presidential campaign as a racial lightning rod, and with each step of the way, as he moved from candidate to office holder, this process only intensified and calcified his public standing and ability to successfully govern. This added an extra burden that made him not just another president that social scientific research has clearly established the parameters of electioneering and governing style for, but also an unknown racially identified president that arguably made even the most mundane and simple tasks, as a candidate and an elected official, the most intriguing and wild adventures ever witnessed in this country.

These dual-layered burdens of a traditional presidential political campaign and the expectations coupled to an unprecedented racial-barrier-breaking presidential campaign placed on Obama were most noticeable and pronounced as he was a candidate in the 2008 Democratic Primary and General Election. In particular, the frequent and devastating racial attacks Obama endured made his campaign and his election victory a remarkable story. There are a myriad of ways to analyze these racial attacks, and many scholars have broached this subject matter. Some of the more common frames of analysis have placed an emphasis on how race and racism operate in our society and how the Obama presidency has been no exception to these racial rules (Wise, 2009 and Bonilla-Silva 2006). Others have analyzed how President Obama's rise to power can be placed in the context of groundbreaking African American men and significant racial benchmarks being met (Nordin, 2012). There are even others that have questioned the value and the meaning of Obama's political success and what his success has meant for African Americans, as well as all Americans in general (Hill, 2009). One area that has been neglected is the role and significance of the executive branch. In particular, what role this branch of national government has historically played for African Americans and for the American public in general. Whether from the standpoint of traditional political science scholarship, or from the perspective of scholars that study race, there is a great deal of work that can be done in this area.

It is critical to understand what choices Obama made and what options were available to him to be able to gain political access and power in his quest. An examination of this process led to the observation that the 2008 Democratic primary and general election were marred by unprecedented racial attacks. To be able to assess the extraordinary nature of these attacks and the racial content of these attacks, I developed a two-prong analysis. One prong moved along the axis of a historical review of presidential attacks, and this pursuit gave form and shape to past and contemporary boundaries for presidential attacks. In particular, within the modern era, a specific form of scholarship has been developed for the study of presidential attacks. Understanding the methodological and theoretical tools of this approach provides a background to be able to evaluate the 2008 campaign as well as how the field of negative presidential campaigning has become an established body of academic work now. The second prong of the analysis was operated fully within the realm of what constitutes race and racism. To be able to establish not just the excessive negativity of the attacks leveled at Obama but the racial weight of these attacks, scholarly work done on race and racism had to be introduced and then applied to the 2008 national elections. In pursuing these two prongs, it became clear that they do not neatly connect at some point, and their greatest utility came from their ability to shed a great deal of light on the 2008 national elections, as well as the Obama presidency. The most intriguing angle that is pursued in this book is the way in which the racist discourse Obama was forced to swim in produced the conditions under which he could govern. This then had a noticeable impact on his development and advocacy of public policy and on his public persona and ability to be a national figurehead.

No one disputed the fact that Obama would be attacked during the Democratic Party presidential primaries in 2008 and then again in the general election for 2008. To what extent these attacks were par for the course for presidential elections or to what extent these attacks went well beyond past campaign etiquette and decorum is what needed to be explored and evaluated. Through the work of James Pfiffner, Jeffery Tulis, Richard Ellis, Mark Dedrick, and Michael Genovese, the basis for examining the informal and formal customs and traditions that have been developed for past political campaigns can be presented, as well as the governing styles of past presidents. Emmett Buell, Jr. and Lee Sigelman's scholarly research on negative political campaigns can be used to support this historical work, and this work provides exceptional insight into how social scientists have approached this subject matter. Utilizing this historical backdrop and the research done on negative campaigning provides a unique filter for assessing the 2008 presidential election. This filter provides insight into how this election provided such a remarkable break from past traditions and customs. In particular, what was uncovered was that these attacks not only stood in stark contrast from previous presidential campaigns, but that the overt and subtle racial discourse injected into this campaign screamed out for a completely different form and basis of analysis than that which is typically employed by scholars. The racial basis of these attacks added a particular type of social, political, and economic weight to them and made them arguably the most insidious and dangerous attacks ever utilized in a presidential campaign. These attacks not surprisingly continued to plague Obama even after the election and became a permanent feature of the climate in which he was able to govern. Firmly establishing a novel political trajectory for a presidential candidate and assessing unusual conditions for governing that no previous President had ever encountered is not enough, and it is necessary to delve deeply into the racial identity of the President, the racial attacks he received, and the racial climate that was built around this presidency. These are necessary ingredients for a careful and complete analysis of the 2008 election and the Obama presidency. To establish the significance of this point, an examination of past presidential campaigns and presidential tenure in office had to be conducted. The historical work done by scholars James Pfiffner, Michael Genovese, Richard Ellis, Mark Dedrick, and Jeffery Tulis will be utilized to illustrate how modern-era presidential campaigns have developed certain customs and traditions and also to show that campaign mode and particular governing styles are inextricably linked. Once campaigns have been completed, the level of decorum extended to sitting Presidents regardless of their political parties has also become firmly entrenched in terms of American customs and traditions. It is from this historical vantage point and through a critical review of the methodological and theoretical tools that have been developed for studying negative political campaigns that an appreciation of what the Obama administration was able to accomplish and what it struggled with can be properly assessed.

Part of this historical vantage point must include the way in which past presidential candidates, as well as office holders, have become immersed in race and racism. Prominent examples from the traditional era, as well as the modern era of American government can be examined that highlight the way in which race and racism has played a role in politics in overt and subtle ways, and how every presidential candidate, as well as office holder, has experienced racism at this level of federal politics. This historical review will help to establish the way in which race and racism have become ingrained in the executive branch and that this feature of the executive branch has mirrored the racial history of the country. The way in which race and racism has manifested in politics also establishes the way in which it goes well beyond the racial identity of the presidential candidates or office holders, and it is not unique to the one African American presidential office holder. Some examples of past presidents' decisions and policy initiatives can be utilized to substantiate this point and help shed light on the ways that race and racism have overtly and subtly had an impact on past Presidents. From the traditional era, government-sanctioned and government-implemented policies towards racial minorities, especially African Americans and Native Americans, provide the most prominent examples of how race and racism have influenced the executive branch. From generic policies, such as slavery policies that supported the forced removal of millions of Africans and the establishment of slavery for these Africans in the Caribbean Islands, North America, and South America, to specific policies, such as the Trail of Tears, there are many easy-to-iden-tify race-based policies. In the modern era, the executive Order from Roosevelt to place Japanese Americans in internment camps, the wars conducted in Southeast Asia in the 1960s and 1970s that were supported by multiple presidents, and even Nixon's use of a "Southern Strategy" to gain White electoral support can all be seen as examples of explicit or implicit race-based executive branch policies and decisions with tan-gible racial consequences. From the standpoint of previous presidential candidates, one could examine the way President George H.W. Bush successfully used a political campaign advertisement on television that featured an African American accused of raping a White woman against his Democratic party opponent (Democratic Governor Michael Dukakis) to successfully win the 2000 presidential election as an example of how potent the use of a racialized image of scary and evil Black men can be for a national election. The way that President George W. Bush used the overt suppression of African American voters in Florida to win the 2000 election provides another example of how a campaign tactic (scrubbing voter lists) can have overt racial consequences (unfairly denying eligible Black voters an opportunity to participate in an election) that ultimately results in political gain (Bush won the national election by virtue of his 537-vote election victory in the state of Florida). Toni Morrison's reference to President Clinton as the "first Black president" provides another exam-ple of how this racialization process might work and what the repercussions of this process might mean for presidential politics.

Another way to examine the way in which candidates running for president have become consumed by racial discourse is when actual racial minorities have run for office. To be able to analyze and understand these racial dynamics, a review of racial minority candidates will be utilized. This type of analysis can shed light on the specific legacy of racial minorities that ran for president, as well as examples of how race and racism directly and indirectly influenced their campaigns. To start this process, the political campaigns of Dick Gregory, Congresswoman Shirley Chisholm, Reverend Al Sharpton, Senator Carol Mosley Braun, and Congresswoman Cynthia McKinney will be briefly examined. Based on Reverend Jesse Jackson's more substantial electoral success in his 1984 and 1988 presidential campaigns, these campaigns will receive more in-depth coverage. With the notable exception of Jackson's campaigns, all of the other presidential campaigns launched by racial minorities were described as fringe campaigns, and all of these campaigns ended with no significant electoral impact. One notable component of these campaigns was the way in which common racial tropes and racial pitfalls had an impact on the campaigns. This was in addition to the regular campaign demands that influenced these campaigns. These campaigns not only contribute to our understanding of the way in which race and racism influences presidential elections but also to the knowledge about the specific historical legacy Obama encountered in his quest for the presidency in 2008. These campaigns provide insights into how racial minority candidates developed their own political brands, how the public responded to their candidacy, and what level of electoral success they were able to achieve. This historical background ties directly into Obama's groundbreaking presidential election and provides an invaluable backdrop to be able to evaluate the Obama presidency.

From this historical backdrop, Obama's attempt to construct a "non-threatening" post-racial identity and his successful marketing of this political brand has a rational political basis. On one level, the fact that every previous African American candidate was not successful and that each of these candidates struggled with perplexing racial dynamics had to be properly addressed by the Obama campaign. On another level, the limited success the Jackson campaigns had in 1984 and 1988 sent potentially at least two contradictory messages. One message could be understood as what an African American liberal candidate could accomplish with limited campaign resources and support. Given the fact that Jackson even won a few states with a majority White population, this could be interpreted as potential acceptance and support for an African American to run as a publicly perceived "race candidate" with a "racial agenda." Another message that could be built on the Jackson legacy would suggest the exact opposite approach. Instead of viewing the potential way in which one's personal racial identity influences the public perception of a highly charged race-based political agenda as a manageable political liability, one could attempt to completely deny the public significance of race and racism and deny holding any race-based political ideology. This latter reading of Jackson's campaign became the basis of Obama's political brand and strategy. It can be shown how Obama's carefully constructed political identity became instrumental for his national success and had a ripple effect on the way he eventually learned to govern, including the decisions he made and the politics for which he advocated. What is most striking is not Obama's extraordinary political success with racial branding, but the fact that the racial assault against him continued unabated. These racial attacks can be shown to not just be unique for Obama, but they virtually erased his self-professed racial identity, and affected public posture towards race-based policies and decisions. These racial attacks could have been more suited for a candidate in the Jackson mold, but the fact that they were utilized against an African American candidate and president who had little in common with Jackson beyond a shared racial identity suggests that a richer and more nuanced analysis can be developed for why and how these attacks continued to be launched against Obama.

The basis of analysis for examining the attacks Obama encountered will first establish the racial nature of these attacks. The second part of the analysis will be devoted to an examination of the impact that these attacks had on Obama's governing style, as well as his development of public policy agenda and policy decisions. For the purposes of this book, I have selected a few of the most significant overt and subtle racial attacks that Obama endured since he launched his first presidential campaign in 2007. The preponderance and consistency of these attacks throughout the Democratic primary elections, as well as throughout the general elections and in both periods of governance for the Obama administration suggests that the all-encompassing nature of racial discourse can also be seen in the operation and maintenance of the executive branch. These attacks help to shed light on questions such as, "Is there a new standard for acceptable attacks on a sitting President and potentially a new and lower standard for acceptable racial etiquette, too?" To be able to address these questions, the work of the previous scholars on the history of attacks in presidential campaigns and attacks leveled at sitting Presidents can be utilized. Depending on how one understands the racial significance of these attacks and the political effectiveness and the social consequences of these attacks, these attacks could also be considered a new low for American politics and the most powerful and long-lasting political attacks ever utilized.

This book will focus on some of the most prominent and popular racist attacks that President Obama encountered in his first presidential campaign in 2008 and during his first term in office. Before examples of these attacks are presented, a discussion of race and racism will be offered. As examples of the racist attacks are presented, an analysis of what constitutes racism will be presented based on the work of Lynn Weber, Joe Feagin, Michael Omi, and Howard Winant. Even though the basis of this book is a specific examination of a sample of the types and forms of racist attacks Obama has encountered, it is also constructed to provide a new entry point for being able to evaluate the Obama presidency, as well as opening doors into how the nexus between race and racism and national politics is examined. A great deal of the scholarship and material that has been produced by the Obama administration has either neglected or misunderstood the significance of these racial assaults. To the extent that these attacks are properly documented and accounted for by some scholars and activist, their work has even been less likely to connect to analysis of the actual development and advocacy of public policy from the Obama administration. Part of the problem has been the fact that the trend started by the Obama presidential campaign to ignore as much as possible overtly race-based issues or positions was extended into the realm of not responding to racial assaults. This trend carried over into his style of governance, and this has not left an easily identifiable roadmap of what racist attacks the Obama administration encountered and how the administration responded to these attacks. To be able to develop the case for the significance of racial assaults leveled at Obama and the impact these attacks had on the Obama presidency, the customs and traditions of previous presidential campaigns and administrations have to be reviewed. From this vantage point the full weight of race and racism can be assessed not just from the standpoint of the executive branch but from how it operates on a daily basis in U.S. society for millions of people categorized as minority races. The inclusion of a racial analysis does not imply a lock box that the Obama administration (or any previous or future presidential administration) has been a prisoner to, but it does provide a way to examine presidential campaigns and executive office holders from outside of the historically grounded methodological and theoretical work that has tended to neglect and misconstrue race and racism. The Obama presidency presents the wholly unprecedented dynamic of not only being the first African American president and the first president to experience direct and personal racial attacks but also being placed in a situation in which the president was expected to address and satisfy the at times conflicting and contradictory yearnings (by virtue of his status as a racial minority) of both the non-White and White racial communities. This situation has to be viewed in the context of a president who made the cornerstone of his political brand a "non-racial" identity. This identity was never articulated in an overtly political fashion, nor was it defended in an overtly political or personal way.

Much of the criticism leveled at President Obama that can be considered racist or race-based has to be understood within a political and social context. This political and social context is based on the view of a primarily White audience that can understand these attacks and is expected to be sympathetic and receptive to these types of racial assaults. The meaning and significance of these race-based challenges to Obama's policies and presidency are primarily based on this audience's ability to glean a particular type of racial meaning and significance from these attacks, not just their ability to find character flaws or weaknesses in his politics or the public policies he pursues. To the extent that these racial attacks are used and considered successful, they can be thought of as a clear indicator of the state of American race relations and, in particular, the way in which the current racial discourse can continue to dominate our lives. The work of Tim Wise will be incorporated into this presentation to illustrate the significance of how a particular form of racial framing provided the backdrop for these attacks, and once placed in this racial frame, these attacks can be considered to be successfully utilized against Obama during the presidential campaigns and during his time in office. Wise's work also helps to distinguish the attacks leveled at Obama as not being the first time that presidential candidates or campaigns were infused with race and racism. The key racial dynamic is the way in which Obama's personal racial identity was intermeshed with racist attacks and racialized public policy debates.

These racial attacks are often described by the dominant media as isolated and insignificant, and rarely is any larger context presented and analyzed to help people to understand these attacks. This position has been largely condoned by Obama and his supporters. In particular, their willingness to not respond to these attacks and draw attention to the racial nature of these attacks suggests that they consider the attacks to be insignificant and unworthy of attention. Another possible interpretation of these attacks is that they are part of a racist discourse the United States has been mired in for hundreds of years now, and there continues to be very little deviation from this racial discourse. To the extent that this analysis is accurate, it would suggest that the continued racist attacks on this one prominent African American might also have very serious implications for millions of racial minorities in the U.S. The approach to these attacks as isolated and insignificant events, as demonstrated by the Obama administration, makes sense only in a "post-racial" context. If we have not reached a "post-racial" moment, then these attacks might more accurately reflect deeply entrenched and persistent patterns of racial identification, meaning, and oppression.

The potential misreading of these racial attacks, based on dominant media reports, highlights the need for and the significance of alternative readings of these "isolated" incidents. A case can be made for many of the attacks that have been leveled at Obama as being based on an overtly racist ideology and cultural traditions and that these attacks have been a part of systemic racial assaults that have been historically launched at African Americans and that they are part of a systemic and institutional form of racism. The fact that most of these racial attacks have primarily come from outspoken conservative White men and that these comments are most often supported and appreciated by largely White audiences suggests that tangible (perceived or real) White benefits can be attached to these attacks. These racial attacks provide an exemplary model of how to understand the growth of and the intensity of the racial assault leveled at President Obama, and they also explain why these attacks continue to be integral to the maintenance and operation of racial discourse in the U.S. It could also be argued that by allowing these racial attacks to go unchallenged, President Obama allowed for the creation and the establishment of a new bar of acceptance of racial intolerance. Put quite simply, if you can say it publicly about the president, then you can certainly say it privately to every Black person now. Every Black person will have to psychologically wrap his or her brain around the fact that even being the highest ranking official in the U.S. will not make one immune from racial assaults! This becomes a form of ongoing racial trauma that the Black community continues to be subjected to and is now magnified by the fact that it was played out on a daily basis on a presidential stage.

To substantiate the significance and the meaning of the attacks leveled at Obama, an examination of past attacks directed at presidents will be presented. Whereas it can be easily established that historically the use of race and racism has never been a part of attacks on presidents while in office, it is less clear how to evaluate the impact and potency of the attacks leveled at Obama compared to the attacks leveled at previous presidents. Through an examination of some previous presidents and some of the more noteworthy attacks on these men, an analysis can be developed and presented. Based on the case made for the significance of race and racism within our society, the validity and applicability of viewing racial assaults as alarming and unsettling can be reviewed. Questions about what attacks have had the most damaging impact on a president and how to assess the accuracy and fairness of the attacks can be posed. The purely political objective and subjective nature of the attacks can also be addressed. The possibility that Obama is simply a case that represents an extension of a long-standing tradition of teeing off on presidents will be examined as well as the possibility that Obama is a case that represents a new, more lethal brand of "presidential exceptionalism" in the realm of public and private attacks.

Ron Walters' work on White Nationalism in the executive branch presents a simple and insightful way to evaluate the Obama adminis-tration. Specifically, Walters' careful analysis of previous Democratic and Republican administration successes and failures in terms of domestic policy that addressed the needs of those that are the most oppressed in the African American community can easily be applied to the same policy areas of the Obama administration. This project encountered a perplex-ing obstacle in terms of not just evaluating President Obama as another President or even another Democratic president, but evaluating his racial identity produces contradictory and confusing trajectories for what poten-tial research can uncover. The most confounding aspect of Obama's racial identity was the onslaught of racial assaults leveled at him before and after he was first elected president in 2008. What became clear is that a simple analysis of domestic policy of successes and failures could not erase this history and declare it insignificant for evaluating his presidency. By the same token, no one could mistakenly attempt to use these racial assaults as an excuse for his failures or even as a justification for his successes.

Another way to explore these racial assaults will be through Walters' White Nationalism theory of how the federal government arrives at public policy decisions, implements these policies, and what these day-to-day operations of the federal government mean for millions of racial minori-ties. Walters' analysis can shed light on what Black political representation means even at the highest level of government and what it also means for an African American to occupy this position of power. Building on the examples of clearly documented racial assaults and the uniqueness of these assaults for a president, one can begin to evaluate what potential openings might be available for public policy. Ron Walters has written numerous texts that have directly or indirectly addressed these questions. To be able to build a case that President Obama's campaign, election, and time in office have racial significance and that racial implications can be observed and evaluated within the context of the executive branch, Walters' work can be used as an invaluable analytical tool. For the purposes of this book, I have selected Walters' text, *White Nationalism, Black Interests: Conservative Public Policy and the Black Community*, and his specific work on White Nationalism and the executive branch will serve as the basis of my analytical approach. This work builds upon and utilizes previous work Walters produced. In particular, as one of the most distinguished and honored political scientists working in the area of African American politics, Walters has continually developed the case for the role that the federal government has in the maintenance and support of White European racial dominance. Walters also makes the case for the existence of oppressive conditions for African Americans and what tactics and strategies might be available to challenge the various forms of oppression non-White communities confront on a daily basis. Of particular concern for Walters is the politics of representation and what the increase in the number of African American and racial minority politicians means for the quality of public policies and decisions that are made that have the greatest impact upon communities of color. It is from this backdrop that the election of the first African American president became one of keen concern and interest for Walters intellectually, as well as personally. Walters' work can be used as a schematic to evaluate and understand Obama's "successes" as well as his "failures." What is most interesting in his work is how Obama has been received, the racial implications of this reception, and the way in which racial attacks against him can be understood from a federal government standpoint.

It is also worth noting that the historical canon that has been built around the executive branch specifically or the federal government could be considered to have limited value at this point. President Obama being the first African American president also means that there have been no other African American or racial minority presidents to compare his performance and public reception to. Comparing him to other presidents will continue to be a source of very intense and complicated debate. In particular, the impact race had on any and all of his decisions, how he was received, and what he was able to accomplish or not accomplish can and will continue to be argued by people inside and outside of academia. Even the limited terrain of trying to compare and contrast the attacks that President Obama has received with those directed at previous presidents is a very delicate and difficult exercise. The particular realm of racial attacks President Obama encountered does present a clear break from previous presidential attacks, and the establishment of this realm must ultimately lead to new theories and a new conceptual framework for understanding the executive branch.

HISTORY OF ATTACKS
ON PRESIDENTS

INTRODUCTION

The history of verbal and written attacks leveled at contestants for the presidency, as well as ones aimed at actual occupants of the White House, is rich. In some of these attacks, detractors and supporters of past presidents have gone to extraordinary lengths to protect favorites and sling mud at opponents. Scholars have conducted a great deal of work on not only tracing this history but also developing and utilizing specific methodological and theoretical tools to analyze these presidential campaigns, as well as what the occupants of the White House have been engaged in and accomplished while in office. It is first from this analysis of the history of campaigns and presidential governing styles that a suitable context for the attacks leveled at President Obama can be built and evaluated. Second, the methodological and theoretical tools used to track and assess past presidents will be examined in the next chapter. To be able to sustain the argument that the attacks on Obama were based on not just a racist discourse but were truly extraordinary in terms of breadth and scope, a historical basis of analysis must be presented and incorporated into the analysis. This chapter will offer a historical context for evaluating the racist attacks leveled at Obama. Then from the vantage point of the historical legacy, a particular type of critique and a set of meaningful questions can be posed for the scholarship done on the Obama presidency.

The first step in placing Obama within the lineage of presidential campaign attacks and attacks leveled at a sitting president is to examine the way in which traditional and customary practices have developed since the first official presidential election of 1789. Since this election, presidential elections have become a staple of American culture and of political discourse. The scholarly work done by James Pfiffner, Jeffery Tulis, Richard Ellis, Mark Dedrick and Michael Genovese will be utilized to provide the historical context for the political campaigns, as well as way to review the governing styles that past and current presidents have embraced. Their historical tracks the ways the Presidency has developed from the Traditional Era of politics into the modern era. As part of this development one can see a more refined, elite era of presidential campaigning and governing style blossom into a deeply personal and intensely competitive era of contemporary presidential politics. To supplement this work, Emmett Buell, Jr., and Lee Sigelman's scholarly research on negative political campaigns will be used in the next chapter to provide insights into how social scientists have approached this subject matter.

HISTORY OF PRESIDENTIAL ATTACKS

It is not surprising that a nation born out of revolt against colonial British rule and steeped in lofty democratic principles would find very sharp and intense political opposition as a common occurrence. With the Declaration of Independence in 1776 and the Constitutional Convention in 1787, the proliferation and solidifying of political ideologies became more and more apparent. One of the clearest divisions was between those who wanted a stronger centralized government (Federalist) and those who were leery of a central government gaining too much power and trusted more power residing within the states (Anti-Federalist). Part of the lingering legacy of the thirteen colonies liberating themselves from the tyrannical power of the King of England was what type of government could be formed and guarantee success, in particular, what form of government could be established that would ensure monarchical rule would not creep back in and plague their new Republic. This fear of monarchical rule was most noticeable in the debates over how much power to grant to the executive branch and how this branch of government would interact with and coexist with the judicial and congressional branches of government. In particular, the division between the advocates of a strong Federalist system, such as James Madison, John Jay, and Alexander Hamilton, and the anti-Federalists, such as Thomas Jefferson, Edmund Randolph, and Patrick Henry, could be seen through this prism of fear and concerns about the executive branch. The legacy of political attacks and responses predates even the first official president, George Washington, who was not even affiliated with a political party. The intensity of these attacks is captured quite well by Michael Genovese's (2001) recitation of the anti-Federalist charges made against the proposed Constitutional structure: "Edmund Randolph of Virginia said the President could be 'the foetus of monarchy,' George Mason saw the presidency as an 'elective monarchy,' and Patrick Henry thought the new presidency 'squints toward monarchy.'" (p. 6). This tension between how much centralized power should exist for the new Republic versus how much power should be retained by the newly formed states could be seen in historical incidents, too. A variety of historical episodes from Bacon's Rebellion to reaction to the Stamp Act to even the War of 1812 highlighted the way in which power was becoming invested in a centralized government and how this process continued to create political divisions and distinct ideologies.

Before a discussion about the history of presidential attacks can be covered, it is also important to note the way in which the nature and style of attacks have developed. Much of the scholarly literature about presidential customs and traditions revolves around two presidential time periods: the "traditional" and the "modern" eras (Pfiffner, 2011; Ellis & Dedrick, 1997). Since these presidential customs and traditions continue to change, it is very important to first capture the key tenets of each era and then illustrate how what was established and accepted in one period began to shift and transform to something slightly or radically different for another time period. This is an extremely salient point for an analysis of presidential campaign attacks as well as attacks leveled at sitting presidents. Most of what we associate with what is customary and traditional for attacks in these areas can be most closely associated with the modern presidency. In fact, even what constitutes a proper and acceptable presidential campaign has undergone a radical transformation from the traditional and to the modern era of the presidency.

To be able to understand the modern meaning of the political attacks leveled at Obama, we must first understand the roots of these attacks that were firmly enshrined in the traditional era that begins with the birth of a new nation in 1776 and the first presidential election of 1788 under the new U.S. Constitution. Starting in 1788, the first two presidential elections not too surprisingly resulted in victories for the popular general of the Colonial army, Washington. Pfiffner (2011) suggests that Washington's presidency set the tone and style for future presidential candidates and office holders by starting with the obvious point: "The Framers provided no formal system for deciding the finalist from whom the electors would choose when they cast their ballots for president" (p. 26). From there Pfiffner suggests that there was not the expectation that opposition parties would develop and there was a clear faith that the men bestowed with the authority to select presidents would make wise decisions. The political culture that developed provided the space for political parties to grow and also set the stage for a very restrained and limited executive branch. This period is referred to as the "traditional presidency" (or traditional era), and it covers presidential campaigns and office holders from 1788 to 1933 (Pfiffner, 2011; Ellis & Dedrick, 1997).

This period is exemplified by the description of presidential campaigns and governance provided by Ellis and Dedrick in their analysis of Jeffrey Tulis' work, "Yet in 'feigning disinterest,' Jeffrey Tulis points out, 'candidates exemplified a public teaching that political campaigns were beneath the dignity of men suited for governance, that honor attended more important activities than campaigns'" (p. 44). Ellis and Dedrick support this claim by describing how a political culture group developed around the idea of the prestige and dignity of the President and the presidency. Campaigning in the 19th century began to be associated with partisan politics and uncouth behavior. Ellis and Dedrick provide insights that illustrate the way in which presidential decorum and etiquette has been developed. Both campaign style and governance were connected to the development of decorum and etiquette, specifically guided by an understanding of the perceived gravitas of the executive Office. Ellis and Dedrick offer numerous examples of presidential campaigns from the 1800s that confirm the potency of this logic. Notable references to this tradition of campaigning can be seen in the way that Ellis and Dedrick describe President Jackson's 1832 campaign as one in which silence and modesty were the highest virtues, and his campaign exemplified this political wisdom. This can also be seen in the way Ellis and Dedrick describe President Harrison's 1840 campaign as being mild in tone and message. The notion of campaigning being demeaning and the idea that a candidate had to retain a nonchalant attitude about public campaigns were among the central tenets of traditional era presidential politics. This insight was bolstered by Ellis and Dedrick's comments about the responsibilities of campaign work by the candidate, who stood above the fray, and by the campaign supporters, who could engage in the mud and muck of electioneering and partisan politics. From these historical anecdotes, one can conclude that the first presidential campaigns and presidential office holders had very modest campaigns when compared to our contemporary standards. These campaigns were dominated by advocates of the candidates, and the responsibilities for successful campaigns were largely in the hands of local and state party structures. Candidates believed that their own humility and virtuous nature were enough for the eligible voting electorate (White, male, adults, and property owners) to process and come to the proper political conclusion.

Cracks begin to appear in this presidential campaign mold and attitude towards presidential governance. An example can be seen in the way that Ellis and Dedrick describe Clay's presidential campaign in 1844: "Clay initially vowed that he would retire quietly to his home because the people 'should be free, impartial, and wholly unbiased by the conduct of a candidate himself,' but he soon broke his pledge of silence, penning several public letters that attempted to clarify his position on the annexation of Texas" (p. 47). It should also be added that James Polk won the 1845 election, and Clay's foray into public campaigning through position-paper letters was not immediately successful. Ellis and Dedrick go on to claim: "For denying the norm, Greeley, much like Douglass and Seymour before him, was denounced as 'the great American office beggar' who believed that 'man should seek office rather than the office the man'" (p. 52). This statement provides a profound way to understand the dignity and reverence associated with the executive Office at that time. This is why Ellis and Dedrick conclude that previous presidential candidates, such as Douglas, Seymour, and Scott, had not lost elections, but that their campaign style, based on a public events and partisan political message, was a critical component of why they lost the elections. This tension between traditional, low-key candidates and those who attempted to present a more public presidential campaign and moved beyond the traditional tactics of front-yard speeches and even letters can be seen in the Greeley, Douglass, and Seymour presidential campaigns from the 1860s and 1870s.

These norms for presidential campaigns spilled over into presidential governance styles and incumbent campaigns. This insight is astutely summarized by Ellis and Dedrick when they state: "Yet at the same time, President Cleveland's behavior in 1888 as well as President Harrison's in 1892 (the first incumbents to be re-nominated by their party since Ulysses Grant in 1872) show that the norms for sitting Presidents were different than those for challengers" (p. 53). This tension between the top office holder in the executive branch and the challengers for this office became more pronounced. Ellis and Dedrick illustrate this point by offering evidence from the New York Times about how unpopular presidential campaigning was at that time. Ellis and Dedrick elaborate on this point by explaining that Presidents Cleveland and Harrison did not actively campaign in a public or partisan fashion. This passage suggests that not only did incumbents conform to the same model of campaigning as new candidates, but that this attitude and practice of campaigning also influenced the governing style of presidents. The belief that presidential decisions should be free from the passions of the public and that governance should be part of a restrained, decisive, and wise decision-making process was common. This complies with the view that an overtly public, bombastic, and shrill campaign style would be antithetical for the office of the presidency.

TRANSITION FROM TRADITIONAL TO MODERN-ERA POLITICS

The transformation from this traditional-era political discourse to the type of political discourse we are currently accustomed to can be seen in a gradual and inconsistent development of presidential elections and executive branch governance. An example of this change can be seen in the campaigns at the end of the 19th Century. Ellis and Dedrick specifically mention two transformative campaigns, and they start with the claim that the 1896 campaign was the most famous in the U.S. history. Ellis and Dedrick then provide the following support for this claim: "It is remembered for Bryan's precedent-shattering speaking tour as well as for the carefully orchestrated and impressive front-porch campaign of William McKinley" (p. 64). What begins to develop is a presidential campaign style that is not limited to the front-porch speeches and also not restrained by an understanding of the dignity of the office and office holder that demanded humility and modesty. Candidates began to more actively campaign nationally, and they more vociferously attacked their opponents and promoted their own campaigns. Public-policy positions and personal testimony became the foundation for campaigns. This shift in campaigning began to take root as candidates discovered more and more national success with the adoption of new campaign tactics and strategies. Ellis and Dedrick suggest that with Bryan and McKinley's campaigns one can see the seeds of the "modern-centered campaigns" being planted.

There was also a noticeable change in the public appetite for this transformation in presidential campaigns, and these campaigns were in essence in tune with and reflected public sentiment. Ellis and Dedrick acknowledge this point in their discussion of Woodrow Wilson's campaigns in the early part of the 20th Century, "In the modern campaign the candidate's persona increasingly was the issue; people wanted to know not just where Wilson stood on the issues but what sort of person he was" (p. 124). Wilson then understood and provided the voting public with a type of presidential character that was desired, presenting himself as a candidate with specific positions on the issues of concern at that time. Tulis (1987) also gives Wilson credit for organizing and participating in the first public-speaking tour for a presidential campaign and successfully using this campaign style to win a presidential election. Wilson, according to Tulis, established not only "the rhetorical presidency" but also "the rhetorical campaign," and for Wilson, the two phenomena were necessarily related. This point is made succinctly by Ellis and Dedrick (1997) when they state that this "rhetorical campaign" was a necessary prerequisite for a "rhetorical presidency." The governing style could reflect a more outward public and partisan campaign style that could remain intact once in office. Wilson revolutionized not just presidential governance but also presidential campaigns, and Ellis and Dedrick present this point when they cover the transition into a period of powerful presidency that become dominated by the personality of the candidate, public exposure of the candidate and campaign, and clarity of the national political message delivered. This marked a distinct departure from previous campaigns in terms of the amount of and type of speaking engagements and the content of the partisan message that was delivered on the campaign trail.

MODERN ERA

The start of the modern era of politics is usually associated with the Roosevelt presidency in the 1930s and 1940s (Pfiffner, 2011; Ellis & Dedrick, 1997). Roosevelt's campaign tactics, as well as his successful governing style, helped to set the stage for a greater awareness and appreciation for the presidency. It was also during Roosevelt's four terms as president that the United States went through the Great Depression, fought in WWII, and became the dominant super power for the globe. This also meant that the modern presidency had been greatly formed and shaped by domestic, as well as global pressure points. Roosevelt represents the modern era of the presidency because of the power he was able to accumulate and the way in which he utilized this power.

Roosevelt's election success in and of itself set the standard for not just obtaining the presidency, but also for retaining the presidential office through an effective governing style. To emphasize this point, Ellis and Dedrick (1997) first suggest, "For the first time, a president was campaigning as actively as a challenger, gave as good as he got, trading partisan barbs before partisan crowds across the nation," and they proudly state, "The president as campaigner had arrived" (p. 85). Ellis and Dedrick place the emphasis not on Roosevelt's first election victory in 1932 but instead on Roosevelt's second election victory. Ellis and Dedrick suggest that his 1936 election is the one that not only solidified Roosevelt's basis of power as president but also established his approach and style as the new modern precedent for presidential elections. Ellis and Dedrick attribute Roosevelt's success to the fact that Hoover's campaign bounced back and forth between an older campaigning style more common in the traditional era and then back into a campaign style firmly grounded in the modern era. Roosevelt's campaign did not suffer from this lack of focus and clarity. This observation, coupled with the fact that Roosevelt was able to accomplish an unprecedented four presidential campaign victories in a row, provided the basis for their analysis. Ellis and Dedrick go on to suggest that Roosevelt's election victories ushered in a new era of election campaigning. Specifically, this idea could be seen in the "historic landslide" loss that Alf Landon experienced and the repudiation of Landon's campaign style and strategy. After the Roosevelt election victories, a return to the more modest, dignified, and simple campaign style would risk permanent election failure. The model Roosevelt developed and nourished set a very high bar for successful presidential election campaigning, and aspects of his campaign tactics and strategies can be seen in current presidential elections. The way in which both incumbents and challengers actively campaign and launch political attacks against each other harkens back to the way Roosevelt engaged his opponents in his campaigns. His utilization of a national campaign strategy can be seen in the way presidential campaigns still attempt to present and cultivate a national image and following. The expectations the public could have for occupants of the White House had shifted, and Roosevelt had found a way to tap into this knowledge and understanding of the electorate.

It is also important to note that Roosevelt's governing style was just as critical a component as his campaigning strategy and tactics for the establishment of what we understand to be the modern era of politics. In particular, Roosevelt developed over his four terms in office a unique approach towards executive branch operations and maintenance. This approach can be seen most clearly in Pfiffner's (2011) observation that, "The Roosevelt era marked the transformation of the presidency from a small, personalized office to a collection of specialized bureaucracies with hundreds of professional staffers" (p. 22). Roosevelt set the standard for a much larger and more powerful executive branch. Roosevelt's legacy can be easily identified in the study of modern-era presidencies, and how momentous this shift was can be seen in the way the executive branch began to operate. Pfiffner reinforces and supports many of the same point Ellis and Dedrick raised about the Roosevelt presidency and the "birth of the modern presidency." Pfiffner specifically highlights the way that the role and responsibility increased with New Deal programs Roosevelt successfully advocated and for which he won congressional support. These programs demanded new government agencies and staff and fundamentally shifted the level and scope of governmental support for social security with the onset of the Great Depression. Based on these insights, it is now important to examine the specific tenets of the modern era of politics that scholars currently study.

The modern era is typically considered to be the time period from 1933 to the current election cycle (Pfiffner, 2011; Ellis & Dedrick, 1997). Even though this era is characterized by the campaign and governing-style trends that are most closely associated with the Roosevelt presidency, it is also important to understand the way in which other presidents and domestic and international events have contributed to the modern era. Pfiffner provides another vantage point to be able to evaluate and understand the modern era of politics. Pfiffner presents the power and authority of the executive branch in terms of its relationship with the congressional branch. Pfiffner specifically suggests that presidential power can be distinguished from congressional power with respect to how much executive branch power has expanded beyond what is proscribed in the Constitution. This growth in executive branch power has been based on what particular presidents have pursued and established for new areas of power and authority. Pfiffner suggests that the congressional and executive branches of government have been engaged in a power struggle for over 200 years. It is from this point that Pfiffner also analyzes the specific victors and victories; this has been especially true for wars and wartime presidents. From the historical analysis of the congressional and executive branch that Pfiffner provides, one can conclude that the Roosevelt presidency was central to understanding of the struggle between these branches of government. By moving beyond Roosevelt's electoral success and governing style, Pfiffner, as well as Ellis and Dedrick, illustrate how the seeds of presidential powers were planted in the Roosevelt presidency. When placed in the larger power struggle between the congressional and executive branches, it becomes easier to appreciate how much the Roosevelt presidency shifted the balance of power towards the executive side.

It is not surprising then that to support this point about presidential powers that Pfiffner first turns to the domestic front and the Roosevelt presidency before moving on to other examples: "In domestic issues, Congress usually dominated the policy-making process, with a few major exceptions" (p. 44). The most useful example Pfiffner provides is based on Roosevelt's signature New Deal legislation. Pfiffner describes this legislation as being instrumental in the way that it "expanded the federal government." From this point Pfiffner moves on to offer a comparison to Lyndon Johnson's Great Society legislation and suggests that Johnson's domestic policy initiatives were on par with Roosevelt's in terms of scope and breath of executive-branch power. This gain in and entrenchment of presidential powers is a critical component for understanding how the modern presidency operates. Pfiffner provides more examples to substantiate these points for modern-era presidents and set the context for how the executive branch operates in the current era. Pfiffner explicitly declares, "Twentieth-century presidential assertiveness came to a high point during 'imperial presidencies' of Lyndon Johnson and Richard Nixon" (p. 168). Pfiffner starts with the Johnson administration and its contribution to these "imperial presidencies" through the way in which he conducted the military campaign in Vietnam during the secret deepening of the U.S. footprint in 1965. Pfiffner then describes Nixon's contribution to the 'imperial presidency' by the way he not only continued U.S. military operations in Vietnam and "resisted congressional efforts" to oversee and control military operations, but also in the way in which Nixon clashed with Congress over executive-branch authority and the criminal behavior associated with the Watergate break-in. These examples begin to illustrate how far presidential power had increased and solidified in the executive branch from the time of the traditional area. The type of campaigning conducted by candidates and the governing style of elected candidates had not just shifted; the actual resources and options available for presidents had also dramatically changed. All of these examples shape and form of the climate in which the Obama presidency existed. Whether it is the debate about the use of drone warfare, National Security Agency domestic spying tactics, a temporary reprieve from extradition for young immigrants, or other executive authority Obama exercised, there is not just a tangible link to the Roosevelt presidency but also a link to Johnson, Nixon, and other presidents who knowingly or unwittingly transformed the presidential boundaries of power.

One of the most noticeable areas of this shift in presidential power can be seen in the actual growth of the executive branch and the level of presidential responsibility and authority that has accompanied this growth. Pfiffner (2011) traces this expanded power of the presidential staff to the actual staffing practices that changed during the Roosevelt presidency: "Although FDR began the modern staffing system in the White House, and Truman organized it more explicitly, it was under Eisenhower that the White House staff became institutionalized" (p. 15). This historical documentation of the modern-era presidents begins to highlight the overall way that power was bestowed upon the executive branch and what specific presidents did to accumulate this power. Pfiffner presents another aspect of this shift through an analysis of the responsibilities and authority of the White House staff in comparison to cabinet secretaries. In particular, Pfiffner draws attention to the fact that in the 1960s and 1970s presidents began to weaken the traditional power, independence, and even access to access to the president that had been historically afforded to cabinet secretaries, and this shift in power resulted in a significant increase in power for White House staffers. On one hand, this shift in the amount of staff and job responsibilities of the executive-branch staff correlates with the shift between traditional and modern-era politics while on the other hand, it also speaks to how much the culture and customs of presidential politics has also shifted. The concentration of power in the White House and the weakening of the ability of cabinet secretaries to shape and direct their areas of responsibility has resulted in more authority residing in the White House. The emphasis on the presidential staff is well understood, and Pfiffner provides a compelling case for the tremendous impact informal advisors and formal staff, such as the Chief of Staff and the National Security Advisors, have for presidential success (Pfiffner, 2011). In particular, in his discussion of the modern era, Pfiffner connects the public success of presidents in areas as diverse as public policy and personal competency and effectiveness to the prominent staff members each president is responsible for selecting. One can begin to appreciate how the Secretary of Agriculture making a simple decision about farm subsidies or Secretary of State making a mundane decision about diplomatic immunity for a fugitive could easily become decisions that could have a direct impact on the public's view of the executive office. These decisions have become more firmly wrapped up in the daily operations of an effectively run executive office. The potential public response to these decisions is just as significant a factor in determining presidential engagement as is any potential benefit or harm these decisions might have for an individual or a group of people. This is why Pfiffner is able to accurately portray the value and significance of the inner circle for presidential staff and advisors in the modern era in comparison to the traditional era. This analysis also provides the link between the shifts in campaign style that have accompanied the change in governing styles for past presidents. The combination of these two components also provides the basis for understanding why such a great emphasis is placed on the modern era of politics. This is especially true for evaluating and studying contemporary presidential campaigns.

What this history of attacks does not explain is the type of racist attacks that were launched at Obama. Why weren't the simple boundaries for campaign decorum adhered to and followed by all of the candidates? Even the standpoint of the modern era and the more combative and abrasive campaign style that had developed would not fully explain the open and vicious use of race against Obama. In hindsight, questions can even be raised about the utility and effectiveness of these racial assaults given the fact that Obama won the election. In that sense, this history and understating of these two eras of presidential elections and governing styles do not enable a casual or expert observer to explain what transpired and why. Possible narratives, such as racial progress, providing the prism to view this election ultimately end up failing, too. Put simply, if the United States has made so much racial progress that an African American man could win the presidency, then how would the negative racist campaigning that transpired be identified and acknowledged? A post-racial electorate should have been turned off by this material, yet this material continued to creep into the election and to be specifically targeted at the one African American running in the race, Obama. Before these questions about race will be addressed, the work of scholars and experts in the field of political campaigns will be examined. The next section will enrich this historical analysis by critically reviewing the methodological tools and theoretical framework that have been utilized for studying presidential campaigns and highlighting the limitations these tools for the 2008 election cycle.

THE SCIENCE OF PRESIDENTIAL ATTACKS

This historical backdrop for past presidencies provides a useful context for understanding contemporary presidential elections and governing styles. Before commentary can be offered about the racial attacks Obama received in the 2008 election, it is worth also adding to this contextual background the actual science utilized for studying negative campaigns in the modern area. From this vantage point an analysis of the current methodological practices and theoretical frameworks can be critically reviewed and applied. In particular, the epigraph at the beginning of this chapter suggests that Buell, Jr. and Sigelman were able to establish through a social-scientific methodology and theoretical framework that the Obama and McCain presidential election in 2008 was the least negative presidential campaign in 48 years (Buell, Jr. and Sigelman, 2008). The rest of this chapter will explore how Buell and Sigelman reached this conclusion, what light their work might be able to specifically shed on the Obama campaign of 2008, and what it might say about research done on negative campaigning in general.

To be able to address basic questions about negative presidential campaigns, such as, "What constitutes as the study of negative campaigns?" "When did they start?" and "Why are they used?" the work of Buell and Sigelman can be utilized to provide a historical framework. Second, they move on to provide a clear methodological and theoretical road map. This road map follows a path that is very similar to the terrain other scholars have developed for the field of negative campaigning in general and also for the more narrow area of negative presidential campaigns. For the first step, Buell and Sigelman establish the historical legacy of negative campaigning by describing the political culture of the first presidential campaigns as one in which non-partisan and large public-speaking events dominated the political landscape. In establishing this point, Buell and Sigelman are also exactly in line with the historical legacy of presidential campaigns that was previously presented through the work of Pfiffner, Ellis, and Dedrick. It is from this shared foundational truth about negative political campaigning in the traditional era that Buell and Sigelman can describe the practice of "cadging" (campaigning for a candidate or a campaign) as being rarely utilized. It was because of the potential consequences of "cadging" for a candidate that Buell and Sigelman believed this work was farmed out to surrogates and could still be an organized part of campaign strategy done out of public sight. This historical observation, coupled with the argument Buell and Sigelman provide for the distinct components of contemporary campaigns, provides the basis for Buell and Sigelman's work on contemporary negative campaigning utilized in presidential elections,

Specifically, Buell and Sigelman offer a variety of rationales for why they selected presidential campaigns from the last 48 years as the basis of their study. First, Buell and Sigelman share the historical observation that since their study starts with the 1960 presidential election between Kennedy and Nixon, then it is important to note for that period, "... most of the technology that figured so importantly in 2008—such as the Internet, satellite downlinks, BlackBerry smartphones, and YouTube—did not exist" (p. 9). Buell and Sigelman's second point highlights the way in which modern technology, social media, and news culture operate on a permanent every-second schedule as well as the abundance of news and information outlets that extends beyond typical news stations and newspapers. The third point that Buell and Sigelman bring to attention is that even within the context of the monumental shifts in political, social, and economic culture starting in the 1960s and on into the 2000s, there was still traditional forms of negative campaigning. These forms can be seen in contemporary political-campaign trends, and Buell and Sigelman highlight this point by drawing attention to the fact that within the 48-year period they cover in their work, they found similar threads of types and styles of negative campaigning. Based on the selection of this specific contemporary period, Buell and Sigelman are then able to present a formulation of what constitutes a negative campaign attack, what are the acceptable targets for negative campaign attacks, and how to measure and evaluate campaign attacks from various presidential election cycles.

For the second step, Buell and Sigelman tackle the issue of how to identify and define negative campaign attacks. Buell and Sigelman start by limiting the scope and breadth of potential negative campaign terrain one might want to try to cover by "...restrict(ing) the use of terms such as smear and mudslinging to the making of 'wild, unsubstantiated charges' of a personal nature," and by using "negative campaigning and negativity as synonyms for attacking or criticizing electoral opponents and their policies" (p. 23). This definition gives form to how one can identify and track negative campaigning, but it also immediately introduces the subjectivity of this field and the potential endless supply of avenues for scholarly research that could be pursued. The first set of definitive questions that could be asked would include, "What is the difference between a 'wild, unsubstantiated charge' and a simple negative attack ad? Who decides if the campaign attack is a smear, mudslinging, or an accurate or fair critique?"

Buell and Sigelman sidestep these more thorny issues about political campaigns by suggesting the following thoughts about accuracy and fairness of attacks. With regards to accuracy of attacks Buell and Sigelman state, "Other things being equal, credible charges pack a bigger punch than patent falsehoods, but the difficulty of determining degrees of untruth in many, if not most, instances is insuperable" (p. 42). Buell and Sigelman reach a similar conclusion for the value of fairness of attacks, but they also acknowledge that determining fairness and accuracy can be extremely difficult. This situation would seem to imply a built-in incentive for politicians to present credible political attack messaging in a campaign, as opposed to messages that are inaccurate and unfair. Regardless of the validity of this claim, it still holds true that a subjective and arbitrary determination would have to be utilized to distinguish political attacks campaigns in this area. Since politicians rarely admit that a political attack is inaccurate or unfair and, by the same token, the politician that is attacked will also usually claim that an attack is inaccurate and unfair, very little ground exists to make objective determinations about the validity of each side's position. Put another way, if the typical frame of reference that is utilized by the mainstream media suggests that attacks are simply partisan accusations, what steps can a scholar take to disentangle and evaluate the packaging and presentation of these attacks?

This is why Buell and Sigelman move in the direction of unlinking these attacks to a partisan filter and continue to build a case for why negative campaigning is a valuable and necessary component of contemporary political discourse. Buell and Sigelman explicitly make this case when they state, "By some accounts, terms such as negative and mudslinging are pejorative and should be replaced with more neutral words, such as attack and criticism" (p. 64). Buell and Sigelman point out that scholars typically make a distinction between personal attacks and differences in public policy, as well as distinctions in the areas of fairness, accuracy, and relevancy of issues and material raised. Once established as an acceptable form of political discourse and an easy-to-identify phenomenon, it is then possibly to proceed with how it can be properly studied and evaluated. Buell and Sigelman proceed into this area of how to study and evaluate this subject matter by first avoiding becoming ensnared in a battle of what constitutes a negative political campaign and then articulating a precise and logical methodological approach. Unfortunately, even if there is agreement as to what constitutes a negative campaign, there is still a great diversity of opinions on what to study in terms of mode and style of delivery, as well as which traffickers of negative campaigning should be studied.

Buell and Sigelman acknowledge these points of contention by offering a few parting key points. They first acknowledge the "methodological thicket (that) has grown up around the subject of negative campaigning," and they suggest that "although almost everyone accepts that negative campaigning means criticizing or attacking a rival candidate, slate, or party during a contest for elected office, no such consensus holds when the same researchers measure the prevalence of negativity in particular campaigns" (p. 66). Buell and Sigelman also draw attention to the fact that scholars have utilized different methodological tools to evaluate the same material, and within a similar area of interest scholars can reach very different results. For presidential elections, this opens the door for research in the area of political actors, such as presidential and vice presidential candidates, political parties, surrogates, organizations, Political Action Committees (PACs), and modes of delivery of negative campaigns, such as mass mailers, television, radio, newspapers, door hangers, phone calls, and flyers. It also means that researchers have substantial potential to use different methodological tools and analytical approaches with the same political material and reach substantially different conclusions.

From this rich array of potential areas to pursue negative campaigning, Buell and Sigelman narrowly focus on campaign statements. Buell and Sigelman present campaign statements as their unit of analysis based on the fact that these statements represent a candidate's position on an issue and can be the basis of a unit of analysis for scholars. From this understanding of campaign statements Buell and Sigelman go on to add the following points: "Every statement focuses on some aspect of the campaign, and we have classified as negative those statements that expressly or implicitly criticize a rival ticket or party" (p. 62). Buell and Sigelman also establish the time frame for the political campaigns and the sources utilized to obtain campaign statements. Buell and Sigelman specifically describe this component of their work as being based on campaign statements in the *New York Times* that are identified and coded in a structured fashion from 1960 to 2008. From this basis Buell and Sigelman can add to this methodological framework the requirement that each item that is coded has to not only make overt reference to the presidential campaign but must be identified within the traditional time period for high campaign season — Labor Day to Election Day. When these pieces are put together, a clear foundation for their methodology is revealed. To the extent that one can argue that the *New York Times* is the most, or one of the most, influential national newspapers, then it would follow that national presidential campaigns would be followed closely by this newspaper. The use of negative campaigning, whether coming directly from a candidate or party or indirectly from a surrogate or organization, would be detected and reported on by the *New York Times*. This would provide an internal filter for relevance and significance for attacks and also provide a certain sense of the mode and feel for a campaign, too.

It is from this methodological foundation that Buell and Sigelman develop the following schematic for translating negative campaigning in the *New York Times* to a quantifiable entity and one that could be useful and valuable for comparing presidential campaigns within a 48-year time period. The basis of this schematic is described in the following way: "For each attack identified in a given item, the coder recorded the identity of the attacker(s) (using a 21-category classification scheme); the identity of the target(s) of the attack (using the same 21 categories); the setting (using an 18-cateory scheme); the topic of the attack (using a 48-category code); and whether an attack employed blame, ridicule, labeling, apposition, and/or charges of lying (coded as a series of binaries)" (p. 43). This approach appears to be very straightforward and aligns well with other quantitative academic work that has been done in the area of negative political campaigning. This type of coding also lends itself to various types of critiques that Buell and Sigelman both seem to first bring attention to, then ultimately dismiss and gloss over. These critiques can be seen in Buell and Sigelman's attempt to clarify and reinforce their points about negative political campaigning and how they define this subject matter in academic fashion.

Buell and Sigelman open the door for certain types of critiques in the way that they understand their own shortcomings and how they anticipate potential critiques they might receive. The most profound example of how Buell and Sigelman do this in their work can be seen in the following passage:

> Of course, not everything said and done during a campaign shows up in the pages of the Times. Accordingly we make no claim to have coded every instance of negative campaigning in the presidential contests of 1960-2008. Like every other study of negative campaigning, ours is source dependent. Moreover, like all news organizations, the Times reports only that news it deems "fit to print" (p. 53).

These comments suggest that since they don't claim to capture every negative campaign, and all research is source dependent, and the New York Times is no better or worse a media source than others, their approach is just one viable and valuable scholarly option. This passage would seem to be an attempt to blunt some of the more obvious critiques that could be leveled at their work: Why newspapers? Why the New York Times? These types of questions would provide a way to critically review Buell and Sigelman's selection of one media source for negative campaigning (e.g., New York Times, Washington Post, Wall Street Journal) or what type of media sources to include (e.g., newspapers, television, radio, internet) or even to what extent their research is exhaustive (What campaign negativity do they miss and what do they detect?). Another more substantial critique could be offered for the actual categories that Buell and Sigelman developed. In particular, each of the areas identified, "identity of attacker(s)," "the setting," "the topic of attack," and "whether an attack employed blame ridicule, labeling, apposition, and/or charges of lying" are all critical components for a study of negative political campaigning, and each of these areas also presents complicated baggage. Even though Buell and Sigelman offer definitive decisions and present plausible justifications for their selection of methodological tools, the unreliable and unstable nature of the subject matter they are studying does not change.

Another way to appreciate the methodological dilemmas is through a critical examination of the theoretical foundation that has been built for the field of political campaigning. The methodological work is only useful to the extent that it can provide meaning for negative presidential campaigning. Negative political campaigning has to be placed in the context of presidential elections, the executive branch, and the significance of how the federal government operates on a daily basis. The pursuit of a theoretical frame to give meaning to this potentially vast terrain for negative campaigning is fraught with pitfalls and contradictions. In particular, the selection by Buell and Sigelman of Stergios Skaperdas and Bernard Grofman's formal model of electoral strategy will serve as the lens to view these theoretical concerns. Buell and Sigelman start with the simple observation necessary for the study of negative campaigning, but this observation opens up more thorny methodological and theoretical questions about the nature and scope of their work. Buell and Sigelman present their work as being based on the "attack propensity score" which measures the frequency of negative political campaigning. Buell and Sigelman then move on to offer their own way to capture these negative campaign attacks by developing a "straightforward measure that divided the number of attack statements by total campaign statements" (p. 31). This included identifying the source of the attacks from inside the campaign, who (or what) the intended target was, and the substance of the material used for the attacks. These observations beg the question of what is being captured and why. A whole series of other questions could flow from this vantage point: Is what is being left out more or less important for political campaigning? Why are negative campaign attacks used in the first place? Does it matter if one campaign is more negative than another? Do these campaign tactics and strategies work in a meaningful vacuum that can be isolated and observed by social scientists? The basic starting point to answer these and many other questions starts with an analysis of the democratic form of government, the two-party political system, and how the executive branch operates in concert with the two other branches of government, judicial and congressional.

Another level of analysis has to be examined. Buell and Sigelman reference this point by first acknowledging the work of other scholars in this field by suggesting, "The negative campaigning literature reflects a general recognition that electoral context influences the decisions of candidates to go negative" (p. 67). The more narrow questions that Buell and Sigelman attempt to address are why the particular type of negative campaigning that is utilized by presidential candidates becomes a part of a campaign in the first place and then, second, how successful the utilization of this negative campaigning for presidential elections has been within the time frame of 1960 to 2008. These areas of inquiry then cannot simply be answered from the methodological standpoint of identifying and tracking the amount of negative campaigning that appears in a particular campaign.

It is from this vantage point that Buell and Sigelman's presentation of their selection of Skaperdas and Grofman's theoretical model can be understood and examined. Buell and Sigelman describe this model as accepting negative campaigning as being "both rational and contingent on candidate standings in the race" (p. 78). Buell and Sigelman go so far as to claim that these decisions are based on a "...cost-benefit analysis of the consequences of attacking a rival" (p. 78). As suggested by the description of this model, the day-to-day conditions of a political campaign are the most critical location for understanding electoral strategy. In other words, it is within the realm of electoral strategy that decisions for negative campaigning are produced, and these calculations are based on a "cost-benefit analysis" of what will move a candidate closer to the goal of an election victory. What is being detected by the methodological tools Buell and Sigelman have developed should be a reflection of the definitive electoral strategies each candidate developed and utilized in the campaigns. This theoretical frame becomes the prism through which each of the presidential campaigns is analyzed and evaluated.

The format for Buell and Sigelman's work closely follows each presidential election from 1960 to 2008. Each section includes the data accumulated for negative campaigns, as well as an analysis at the end of each section that is based on the Skaperdas and Grofman's model. The elasticity of this model is on full display as Buell and Sigelman apply to it all of the particularities that can appear in an election. According to Buell and Sigelman, one example where this can be seen is in the way that Skaperdas and Grofman's model can incorporate third-party challengers. The logic of negative campaigns shifts when third-party candidates enter presidential elections, and, to the extent that these candidates become "viable," the two mainstream party candidates adjust accordingly. The overarching logic for the approach taken by Buell and Sigelman is based on the same shared principle that the Skaperdas and Grofman model utilizes: "Presidential candidates have a more accurate understanding of how well they are doing during the campaign than how they will do on Election Day" (p. 54). Put simply, the Skaperdas and Grofman model can anticipate and incorporate when and how three-way races, as well as two-party races, will utilize negative campaigning. The thrust of the utility of this model for Buell and Sigelman as a heuristic device can be seen at the end of their discussion of negative campaigning in each of the presidential elections.

Buell and Sigelman are able to conclude that the Skaperdas-Grofman model was less useful in providing an analysis of negative campaigning for the 1976 presidential election than it was for the 1968 election. The basis for this critique comes from the observation by Buell and Sigelman that "an attacker loses as well as gains by going negative" and how they apply this to the success and failures in Carter's and Ford's campaigns (p. 124). This can also be found in their discussion of the 1964, 1972, and 1984 presidential elections. In particular, Buell and Sigelman first suggest,

"Goldwater, McGovern, and Mondale fought ferociously against pro-hibitively favored opponents" (p. 124). The next logical step that flows from Buell and Sigelman's analytical framework for underdog candidates and negative campaigning would be based on the logic that "favored nominees waged a less negative campaign in every instance" (p. 124). To buttress this point, in these three election examples not only did the candidates that were favored ultimately win, but it can be documented and verified that they engaged in substantially less negative campaigning. These examples illustrate the way in which the methodological tools developed by Buell and Sigelman and their selection of the Skaperdas-Grofman model as the analytical basis of their work are inextricably linked.

CONCLUSION

It is worth now returning to the previous concerns about the methodological and theoretical basis for research conducted on negative political campaigning, in particular, questions such as, "What happens to negative campaigning that is not detected by mainstream media or not delivered by appropriate actors?" Questions could be posed specifically for how the Skaperdas-Grofman model operates: "What happens to negative campaigning that is not detected or supported by this model? What happens to entire campaigns that do not follow the logic of this model? How is race and racism detected by this model?" Instead of working through each of the claims Buell and Sigelman make based on this analytical model or even questioning what data they collected and how they collected this data through a critical review of each section of their work, it is more useful and effective to simply turn to one particular election. From the vantage point of the 2008 Democratic primary and general election, Buell and Sigelman's work can be evaluated. The questions that have been previously posed will serve as the basis of the next section, and the applicability of Buell and Sigelman's work can be evaluated from the standpoint of Obama's campaign. With the introduction of an analysis of race and racism, a case will be made for the way the science of evaluating presidential campaigns and governing style does not provide adequate tools for evaluating the 2008 presidential campaign and subsequent governing style of Obama. The specific methodological and theoretical steps that Buell and Sigelman utilized that ultimately led to their conclusion about the 2008 presidential election being the least negative (epigraph at beginning of this chapter) will be shown to be inadequate when placed in the context of racial discourse.

FROM RUN, JESSE, RUN TO NO DRAMA OBAMA

Cornel West's rage against President Barack Obama evokes that kind of venom. He has accused Obama of political minstrelsy, calling him a "Rockefeller Republican in blackface"; taunted him as a "brown-faced Clinton"; and derided him as a "neoliberal opportunist." In 2011, West and I were both speakers at a black newspaper conference in Chicago. During a private conversation, West asked how I escaped being dubbed an "Obama hater" when I was just as critical of the president as he was. I shared my three-part formula for discussing Obama before black audiences: Start with love for the man and pride in his epic achievement; focus on the unprecedented acrimony he faces as the nation's first black executive; and target his missteps and failures. No matter how vehemently I disagree with Obama, I respect him as a man wrestling with an incredibly difficult opportunity to shape history. West looked into my eyes, sighed, and said: "Well, I guess that's the difference between me and you. I don't respect the brother at all" (Dyson, 2015).

INTRODUCTION

The previous chapter provided a glimpse into the history of negative campaigning in presidential elections, as well as the methodological and theoretical approaches scholars have utilized for this field. The historical account of past presidencies follows the same race-neutral logic of the science of studying negative campaigning in presidential elections. On one level, presidential campaigns and terms in office appear to be the safe terrain of elderly White gentlemen, and they are completely devoid of the taint of race. Presidential discourse from the traditional era, as well as the modern era, is based on the prestige and dignity of the office and the power that is associated with this office. The candidates for president, as well as the actual presidential officer holders, have always been immersed in overtly and subtle forms of race and racism. At no point have presidential candidates or office holders been above the fray on racial matters or simply driven by more pure and honest motives. The way in which race and racism have come to be a part of the executive branch is not a new phenomenon, and it did not start with the Obama campaign in 2008. This phenomenon is not limited to the racial identity of the presidential candidates or office holders. Race and racism have historically seeped into the executive branch in many ways, and Obama was not the first presidential candidate and office holder to confront profound racial quandaries on a personal level, as well as on a level of policy decisions and legislative agenda.

These racial dilemmas extend beyond the boundaries of Obama's personal identity, and they are certainly engrained in the fabric of American society. To substantiate this point, some of the ways that race and racism have overtly and subtly influenced presidential governing styles and policy initiatives will be reviewed. Based on this historical analysis, an argument can be made for the unique and added character of the racialized executive branch Obama has inherited based on his own racial identity. Thus, the fact that Obama is a racial minority has added a substantially new development to the racialized nature of the executive branch. Obama was not only a target of racial attacks unlike any other president, but he was literally governed by the same decisions he made for racial minorities. A large segment of the public expected him to identify with his race and expected some connection between this racial identification and his policies and governing style. The part of these racial dynamics that received the bulk of coverage in this work is the specific way that racial attacks on Obama were distinct and destructive. These attacks impacted his development and advocacy for policy, as well as his public governing style. To be able to appreciate these racial dynamics, a review of racial minority candidates can be conducted, and this analysis can shed light on the specific legacy of racial minorities running for the most powerful position in the world. In particular, the political campaigns of Dick Gregory, Congresswoman Shirley Chisholm, Reverend Al Sharpton, Senator Carol Mosley Braun, and Congresswoman Cynthia McKinney will be briefly examined before Reverend Jesse Jackson's 1984 and 1988 political campaigns will be reviewed in a more extensive fashion. Most of these campaigns were considered marginal efforts, and all of these campaigns ended in defeat. The way in which common racial tropes and racial pitfalls had an impact on the campaigns, as well as the way the standard campaign demands influenced these campaigns impacted will be addressed. An examination of these campaigns contributes to an understanding of the way in which race and racism influences presidential elections. Whether it is through references to race-based policy, the amount of racial minorities allowed to vote in an election, or even the way in which a White president's identity becomes racialized, this can be seen as linked to the way in which African Americans have struggled to run for the presidency.

EXAMPLES OF RACE AND RACISM IN PRESIDENTIAL POLITICS

It is not unusual for overt and subtle forms of racism to enter into a presidential campaign. Whether in specific policy positions or personal comments, the fact that the U.S., prior to Obama, had only presidents of European ancestry does not mean that race and racism were not central components of many presidential elections, nor that these elements were not influential during the time in office. From the traditional era examples include the genocidal policies developed for Native Americans or the oppressive policies put into place for Africans brought to the U.S. as slaves. Specific actions and policy initiatives from presidents had a dramatic impact on these two racial groups historically. President Andrew Jackson's support of the Indian Removal Act of 1830 led to the Trail of Tears that forced the removal of Native Americans from their land by the U.S. military and resulted in the deaths of thousands of Native Americans. The first Fugitive Slave Act of 1793 was passed during the time of the first president of the United States, George Washington, the president considered by many to be the "father of the country." He is also a president who owned slaves and supported openly racist legislation.

From the modern era, specific presidential candidates support for issues and policies that had direct or indirect racial connotations is also very easy to identify. From President Roosevelt's support of executive Order 9066 that placed thousands of Japanese Americans in internment camps to President Richard Nixon's use of a "Southern Strategy" to gain White electoral support for the Republican Party, this era has also been rich with overt and subtle forms of racism in presidential campaigns, as well as during time in office. In terms of African American experience in this country, presidential candidates' and office holders' support for segregation or integration was the historical litmus test for racial hostility and harm. This policy was also a significant test for White electoral support, and in particular regions, like the South, it was the most important consideration for a majority of eligible White voters. Other racial minorities, Latinos, Asian Americans, and Native Americans also saw many of their community concerns not properly addressed, as well as having a response to their issues from the federal government that appeared to display outright hostility, avoidance, or neglect by some presidential candidates and office holders. This negative attitude could be seen in policy debates and presidential decisions about immigration reform under President

Ronald Reagan or the ongoing dispute Native Americans have had with the creation and operations of the Bureau of Indian Affairs that is a part of the Department of the Interior in the federal government or even in the brutal and horrific wars conducted in Southeast Asia in the 1960s and 1970s that had a dramatic impact on the countries the U.S. invaded and/or bombed, such as Vietnam, Laos, and Cambodia, as well as on the Asian American communities in the U.S.

More contemporary examples of race and racism in the executive branch could be expanded to include political campaign advertisements, such as the infamous "Willie Horton" commercial, the way in which a president can become "Black," as well as the actual role African American voters can have in a presidential election. This campaign advertisement featured a convicted felon, Willie Horton, who was in prison for life without parole, and it was utilized by then candidate George H. W. Bush to defeat his Democratic opponent, Governor Michael Dukakis, in the 1988 presidential election. Horton had been released for a weekend furlough based on a Massachusetts limited-release-time prison program. During one of these furlough-release periods Horton committed armed robbery and rape, and his victim was a White woman. The way in which this African American man was featured in a political advertisement by the Bush campaign was described in the following way by David A. Love (2013): "Willie Horton upended the (presidential) race and represented a new low in race-card politics and the manipulation of white fear of black criminality—and an irrational and visceral hatred of black people in general to win elections" (p. 1). The fact that Dukakis was a White man did not soften the racial blow or diminish the impact race and racism had in this presidential election. As described by Love, this political-campaign advertisement was used as a way to tie Dukakis to the most feared and dangerous element within the African American: "In a similar fashion as the racist attacks on Obama will be presented, the historical context for this advertisement provides the basis for understanding the racial meaning and impact: Atwater's Horton ad played on the narrative of the menacing black man who rapes white women, of which rumors often led to race riots and the lynching of black men under the Jim Crow era"

(p. 1). Love goes on to claim that, "This ad represented the ultimate in the Southern Strategy, that is, the Republican Party's raw, unabashed appeals to white Southerners through the invocation of white-skin solidarity and fear of people of color" (p. 1). In this case, the use of highly charged racist political advertisement was quite effective, and it played an integral role in Bush's 1988 election victory.

The way in which race and racism are introduced to presidential politics is not limited to Republican attack commercials against their Democratic opponents. The way in which President Bill Clinton was racialized can be seen in Suzy Hansen's (2002) presentation of Toni Morrison's remarkable assessment of Clinton: In her now-famous defense of a scandal-plagued Bill Clinton, Nobel Prize winner Toni Morrison went so far as to call him "our first black president. Blacker than any actual black person who could ever be elected in our children's lifetime." "Clinton," Morrison wrote in her 1998 *New Yorker* essay, "displays almost every trope of blackness: single-parent household, born poor, working-class, saxophone-playing, McDonald's-and-junk-food-loving boy from Arkansas." (Hansen, 2002, p. 1) Part of this assessment was based on the fact that Clinton was quite often treated unfairly and attacked unmercifully by conservative and Republican opponents. Clinton's "victimhood" resonated within the African American community. The history of racial oppression and dis-crimination that African Americans experienced was one of the reasons why this community was more receptive and sympathetic to Clinton's plight. Morrison builds on the nature of the attack and the response from the African American community by offering a way to understand Clinton's "blackened" background. Morrison then uses elements of Clinton's upbringing (poor, single mother, saxophone playing, etc.) to not only substantiate his "blackness," but to also be able to explain the viciousness and unrelenting nature of the attacks Clinton faced while in office (unprecedented accusations and investigations into private mat-ters). To the extent then that these attacks could connect to Clinton's overtly "Black" characteristics and upbringing, then a particular type of racial logic could be applied to it and successfully explain what was transpiring during the Clinton presidency. Even though Clinton is a White man, it did not preclude his presidency from confronting overt and subtle forms of racism. Morrison's comments arguable made visible many of the sentiments circulating within the African American community. African American support of Clinton not only manifested in very higher voter support for both the 1992 and 1996 presidential elections but also in the way in which polls consistently registered high African American support for Clinton, even after the Monica Lewinsky scandal and the unsuccessful attempt to impeachment Clinton. It is also important to note that the way in which the Clinton presidency was racialized in this respect did not necessarily have any connection to the policies and positions that his administration advocated. In particular, it could be argued that Clinton's support of welfare reform, his "mend it, don't end it" position on affirmative action, and the administration's criminal justice legislation were all overtly hostile policies for large segments of the African American community.

The amount of African American voters also plays a vital role in presidential elections. It can make the difference in presidential election victories, such as Kennedy in 1960 and Carter in 1976, as well as presidential defeats, such as Gore in 2000 and Kerry in 2004. The appeal to African Americans and their actual participation in elections is inextricably linked to racial dynamics. Two prominent examples of this process can be found in the suppression of African American votes in Florida during the 2000 presidential election. In this election Republican Texas Governor George W. Bush defeated his Democratic Party challenger, Vice President Al Gore. Bush's razor-thin victory rested upon winning the state of Florida, and conveniently his brother, Jeb Bush, was the governor of Florida, and the Republican Party controlled the Secretary of State Office's that oversaw the state election. His Democratic Party opponent ultimately contested the election all the way up to the Supreme Court, and the Supreme Court validated the Secretary of State's election decision. This gave Bush the 537-vote victory in Florida and an extra 25 Electoral College votes that moved him ahead of Gore by 5 votes, 271 to 266. The suppression of African American votes nationally, as well as specifically in Florida, played a prominent role in the election victory for Bush. Greg Palast (2004) emphasizes this point by claiming, "1.9 million Americans cast ballots that no one counted." 'Spoiled votes' is the technical term. The pile of ballots left to rot had a distinctly dark hue: About one million of them—half of the rejected ballots—were cast by African Americans although black voters make up only 12 percent of the electorate" (p. 32). Even though the exact figure of "spoiled votes" might not ever be agreed upon or even the percentage of these votes that were cast by African Americans, it is not disputed that a significant number of African American votes were suppressed.

One element of this suppression Palast describes in his discussion of Gadsden County in Florida is that it had "the highest percentage of black voters in the state—and the highest spoilage rate. One in 8 votes cast there in 2000 was never counted. Many voters wrote in 'Al Gore.' Optical reading machines rejected these because 'Al' is a 'stray mark'" (p. 32). At first glance this can be understood as standard electoral monitoring and that it is devoid of any racial connotation. When Palast properly places in this in the context of what transpired in other Florida counties, this practice begins to take on a very different level of significance and meaning. Palast compares these results to other areas: In "neighboring Tallahassee, the capital, vote spoilage was nearly zip; every vote counted." This leads to the racial context and conclusion: "The difference? In Tallahassee's white-majority county, voters placed their ballots directly into optical scanners. If they added a stray mark, they received another ballot with instructions to correct it" (p. 33). This examination of commonplace election processes not only highlights the racial element component embedded in it but also the direct way this process can impact local, state, and even national elections.

Another example of how what appeared to be a standard process of cleaning up voter rolls became deeply mired in a racist process can also be seen in what transpired during the 2000 presidential elections in Florida. Palast describes this process in an interview by first establishing the procedure that was undertaken by the state of Florida: "Five months before the election, Florida Secretary of State Katherine Harris ordered the removal of 57,700 names from Florida's voter rolls on grounds that they were felons. Voter rolls contain the names of all eligible, registered voters. If you're not on the list, you don't get to vote" (p. 17). This might not seem to be an unusual or nefarious process, but Palast points out that he "discovered that at minimum, 90.2 percent of the people were completely innocent of any crime—except for being African American." Palast then provides this observation to support his point that the race of the voter was part of the data that was available to review. This statistic radically transforms the process of cleaning the voter rolls from supposed "dead weight" (people who should be removed from the voter rolls) to one which is not just politically organized (scrubbing the names of potential Democratic voters) to one that is part of an overtly racist practice that is firmly entrenched in a historical racist discourse (the suppression of African American voters through legal and illegal means). With the vast majority of African Americans voting Democratic and especially in the 2000 election for Al Gore, it can be concluded that even a smaller portion of this vote could have dramatic consequences. Only about 500 African American voters would have been needed to deliver Florida state and the national presidential elections to Gore and the Democratic party. With this extremely unusual circumstance of the Florida election being decided by only 537 votes and the national election going to the candidate that won Florida, it can be concluded that race and racism played a central role in determining the 2000 presidential winner. As with the previously mentioned examples of race and racism in presidential elections, this example involved a White man. Even though Al Gore is a White man, this did not stop or preclude his presidential bid from becoming deeply mired in a racist discourse and in racist practices. The fact that he had no control over these racial dynamics provides more credence for the way in which race and racism continue to influence and impact presidential elections, as well as public-policy decisions. This process can be seen in the African Americans that have run for president, and the way in which race and racism seeps into these presidential campaigns can seem to be more rudimentary and predictable, as well as consequential and devastating.

PAST AFRICAN AMERICAN PRESIDENTIAL CANDIDATES

Obama was not the first African American to run for president, nor was he the first person of color to run for president. It is important to acknowledge the impact that race and racism has had in the experience of previous candidates of color in running for president. The fact that before Obama all of the previous occupants of the White House had been White men does not mean that these historical results were solely based on racism and that the election of Obama ushered in the end of a racist practice of electing only White men to be president of the U.S. Other racial minorities have run for president before Obama, and all of these candidates have lost in the primaries as candidates for one of the two major parties, or they lost in the general election as independent candidates. The idea that Obama was the first racial minority to run for president who had a "legitimate" chance to win has been widely circulated. This raises questions about what made the other racial minority candidates not "legitimate" and to what extent race and racism has factored into the way that previous racial minority candidates were seen and treated during the time of their respective campaigns. Other questions could be asked about to what extent race or other factors impacted these candidates' decisions to run for president, how did they conducted their presidential campaigns, and ultimately why they failed are all worthwhile questions to explore. It can be shown that many of the lessons that can be gleaned from the successful Obama campaign were part of a greater narrative that had already been well established in previous racial minority campaigns. To delve into these questions, the political campaigns of Dick Gregory, Congresswoman Shirley Chisholm, Reverend Al Sharpton, Senator Carol Mosley Braun, and Congresswoman Cynthia McKinney will be briefly examined, before Reverend Jesse Jackson's 1984 and 1988 political campaigns will be reviewed in a more extensive fashion.

The earliest presidential campaign for an African American was launched by comedian and civil rights activist Dick Gregory. Quite often this campaign is dismissed as not a serious bid for the presidency, and his candidacy is characterized as an attempt to offer a "protest vote" option or simply as a way to raise political awareness. The following description of his campaign that was presented by democracy8888 in the *Daily Kos* highlights the inherent marginality of his effort: "In 1968, Dick Gregory again tried his hand at politics, this time as the presidential nominee for the Freedom & Peace Party, a splinter group from the Peace & Freedom Party, a party that emerged out of the civil rights and anti-war movements" (democracy8888, 2008, p. 1). This is why democracy888 suggests that it was not surprising that Gregory ran on a ticket based on a splinter group from an already marginal political party and that he would not fare well in terms of electoral politics measurement for success: "Gregory earned more than 47,000 votes in the election, or .06% of the total" (p. 1). Even within this prism of a fringe candidate representing a politically insignificant party, it is worth noting that some of the central themes of his campaign at face value were not race based and not radical propositions. One example can be seen in the way that democracy8888 describes the type of governmental reform Gregory offered for the public sector: "Gregory suggested reforms for fire and police departments as well as the criminal justice system and the courts" (p. 1). More details are provided by democracy8888 in the next line when direct quotation from Gregory is utilized: "'As president,' he wrote, 'I will make every effort to free the court system from political ties'" (p. 1). A specific example was given when Gregory mentions that he "will seek federal legislation to rule out the concept of judgeship by political appointment" (p. 1). It can be argued that this is not only still a viable political issue but that this type of reform has been advocated at times by mainstream political candidates, both Democrats and Republicans. The fact that Gregory did not present this proposal in an explicitly racial fashion is important to acknowledge. One could even argue that Obama's mainstream campaign packaged some liberal reforms that might have a direct or indirect impact on racial minority communities in a "non-racial" fashion.

These same themes are articulated in the following passage about Gregory in a post from democracy8888: "America must re-evaluate what is meant by developing 'stronger' nations. A nation that is well equipped militarily, yet plagued with disease, hunger and ignorance, is not really strong" (2008, p. 1). This passage could be seen as almost identical to Reverend Jackson's speech, and it clearly expresses a sentiment that continues to hold currency in today's political world. This argument is utilized by mainstream politicians on a regular basis, whether from a traditional liberal Democratic Party standpoint or a contemporary Libertarian position. Gregory did not preface this comment by declaring the state of African Americans or by making the link between a less militarized nation and the potential benefits for racial minorities. These points suggest that the self-inflicted marginality of the political party Gregory associated with quite possibility superseded the legitimate and/or radical nature of any his policy planks or his political philosophy or even his lack of political experience and knowledge.

The level of marginality of African American candidates had not shifted four years later when Congresswoman Shirley Chisholm ran for president. Congresswoman Chisholm at first glance appeared to have a more appealing political resume to run for president: She was a current member of Congress, she was affiliated with one of the two major political parties (Democrat), and her political ideas and philosophy seemed to fall safely within the boundaries of acceptable political discourse. Jo Freeman (2005), feminist, political activist, and political scientist, describes the setting for this candidacy in the following way: "In July of 1971 Shirley Chisholm, Member of Congress from New York's Twelfth District, began to explore the possibility of running for president. When she formally announced her candidacy the following January 25, she became the first woman and the first African American to seek the nomination of the Democratic Party for the nation's highest office" (p. 1). It is striking then to move from the novelty of this political backdrop to the reality of the campaign life Chisholm confronted and the political results she was able to muster. This is succinctly presented in the following passage from Freeman's 2005 work: "In the 1972 Democratic presidential primary, she fought an uphill battle against George McGovern" (p. 1). Freeman goes on to state, "She survived three assassination attempts during the campaign," and "she campaigned in 12 states and won the Louisiana, Mississippi, and New Jersey primaries, earning 152 delegates" (p. 1). Freeman also includes the following insight: "At the Democratic National Convention, as a symbolic gesture, McGovern opponent Hubert H. Humphrey released his black delegates to Chisholm, giving her a total of 152 first-ballot votes for the nomination" (p. 1). These anecdotes suggest more tangible political results than the Gregory campaign was able to accomplish, but they also provide a glimpse into the degree of difficulty minority candidates face in presidential elections. On one level her policies, positions and advocacy work demonstrate a commitment to racial and gender justice. Besides opposing the military draft, Chisholm advocated for increased support for social services, and she even sponsored a child care bill that was eventually vetoed by Richard Nixon. This does not suggest a radical politician or presidential candidate, but her campaign became a lightning rod for various forms of political mayhem, including assassination attempts. President Nixon's description of her child care bill was even referred to as "the Sovietization of American children" (Gandy, 2005, p. 1). Chisholm's support for this legislation was not based on a commitment to the Communist Manifesto, nor was it presented as part of Black Power or Feminist political movements and ideology. On political grounds, Chisholm's presentation of this child care bill, as well as her support of other political causes were channeled through the simple prism of those most in need in our society and how these communities are often neglected. Her congressional district in New York was an area that arguably demanded the type of political positions and legislation Chisholm advocated and that she served her constituency quite well. The level of support for social services and, specifically, government-supported childcare to help working women and low-to-moderate income families are all also still relevant political-policy matters, and they are all issues that a new generation of politicians continue to find sympathy for and form solidarity with Chisholm's positions and work. This then begs the questions of how much of the political fire that ensued in and around Chisholm's campaign was based on her gender and racial identity and not her specific political philosophy or legislative agenda. Would her campaign be considered so marginal and produce such inconsequential traditional political gains if her social location were different?

The next two campaigns that are reviewed come after Jesse Jackson's campaigns in the 1980s and have the added advantage of this historical legacy of African American candidates to draw upon. Both candidates, Senator Carol Mosley Braun and Reverend Al Sharpton, ran for the 2004 Democratic Party nomination and lost. They were also the two African American candidates running in this presidential election. Besides these similarities, their campaign style, political history, and political philosophies were substantially different. Senator Mosley Braun had substantial political experience and was one of only two African American senators elected since the Reconstruction period, and she was only the second African American woman to run for the presidential nomination for a major political party. This political heft did not translate to any more substantial electoral success than any other African American political candidates for presidency had achieved. In fact, her campaign results were described in the following manner by Lauren Johnston (2004): "Braun never broke out of single digits in national and state polls and failed to qualify for several state ballots" (p. 1). This coupled with the fact that she was not able to gain political traction in the traditional areas doomed her campaign. Johnston (2004) describes Braun's inadequate fundraising efforts as follows: "And though she had been endorsed by two influential women's groups—the National Organization for Women and the National Women's Political Caucus—that support failed to translate into financial support. Braun struggled to raise money while running up thousands of dollars in debt" (p. 2). Despite what appears at first glance to be a distinct level of political progression from Congresswoman Chisholm to Senator Mosley Braun along with the political strength that should be afforded a campaign from these two different levels, Mosley Braun's campaign did not translate into any more significant political results. Senator Mosley Braun abandoned her presidential bid before the first scheduled primary or caucus, and Johnston presents this political fact in the following manner: "Braun is the second Democratic presidential candidate to pull out of the race before the start of voting on Jan. 19 with the Iowa caucuses" (p. 2). The paradox of a politically well positioned senator from Illinois running for president in 2004 not being able to produce substantially better results than a Congresswoman from a much smaller congressional district in New York can be explained by potentially many other factors. Campaign organization, lack of financial funds raised, even political will and character could be offered as explanations why Senator Mosley Braun did not do as well as Congresswoman Chisholm. According to Johnston, what was abundantly clear about Senator Mosley Braun's campaign was the fact that it was barely noticeable: "She leaves the race after having little impact on it, except for some bright moments in debates. Braun often stressed during the campaign that she was running for president because it was time to 'take the 'Men Only' sign off the White House door'" (p. 1). This became a distinct point of departure from Congresswoman Chisholm who competed in 12 Democratic state elections, won a few elections, and gained delegates. Her campaign was also different than Reverend Al Sharpton's presidential bid, and they were both in competition for the 2004 Democratic Party Nomination.

Reverend Al Sharpton's 2004 presidential campaign is remarkable in the way that he openly ran as African American candidate on issues associated with the African American community. His campaign also provides a lens to view the other African American presidential bids. As a well known and established civil rights leader, Sharpton is still associated with Tawana Brawley's false accusations of being raped by multiple White men in 1987. Sharpton was one of her most prominent public supporters, and he led an active campaign to defend her and vilify some of the men she falsely accused of raping her. The controversy that was created by the grand jury deciding to not charge any of these men and revealing the lack of merit of Brawley's accusation continues to leave a stain on Sharpton's image today. From Amadou Diallo to Sean Bell to the U.S. Navy bombing test site in Vieques, Puerto Rico, to the Jenna Six to most recently Trayvon Martin, Sharpton has a very deep and rich history of being a civil rights leader on the most profound and significant cases of injustice for communities of color. Sharpton's history in some respects made his campaign platform and positions on issues irrelevant for how his campaign would be received and understood.

Tommy Llamas describes how Sharpton was openly presented as an unapologetic and unashamed Black candidate running on Black issues, as his specific campaign revolved around these key planks and his desire to see changes in the Democratic Party platform. Llamas (2004) makes this case by first stating, "At this point Sharpton wants the Democratic Party to adopt his 'urban agenda' and that agenda, says Sharpton, will range from jobs and health care for the poor to addressing the issue of 'police misconduct'" (p. 1). Llamas concludes that, "For Sharpton to leave the race, the party would have to agree to make the 'urban agenda' part of their national platform going into the general election" (p. 1). Given what could be considered common progressive ideological points and historically sound Democratic Party positions, Sharpton received a scathing and sarcastic attack from Clarence Page, a fellow African American man and a syndicated columnist for the *Chicago Tribune*. Page's article, "What a Friend Bush Has in the Rev. Al Sharpton," provides a potent reminder of the dilemmas and the contradictions embedded into the process of any racial minority running for president in the United States. Page (2004) starts by claiming that "As a master of spin, Sharpton put a happy face on these little victories as if they actually meant something. He's not about to let a little matter like a lack of votes prevent him from declaring victory" (p. 1). This amusing quip is based on African American candidates' inability to mount successful traditional campaigns and achieve tangible electoral goals. Based on the previous history of other African American candidates, including ones that had extensive political experience and held powerful elected positions, it would not be surprising that Sharpton would meet the same fate as most of these candidates. In fact, even his African American counterpart in this race, Mosley Braun, did not last as long in the Democratic Primary. A case could be made for the value and the contribution of "protest" or "political awareness" campaigns. Certainly the campaigns of Gregory, Chisholm, and Jackson could all be offered as examples of unsuccessful bids for the presidency but also campaigns that contributed to the development and the molding of political ideas and campaign tactics and strategies that are still utilized today.

Page then makes a very telling pivot from his point about the inevitable failure of traditional campaigns to discussing specific weakness for Sharpton as an African American candidate and his appeal to African

Americans. Page conveniently presents Sharpton's assumed appeal for the African American community as the most significant benchmark for determining his success: "South Carolina was a telling blow. With its large black population, large enough to account for about half the Democratic turnout, Sharpton had positioned South Carolina to be his strongest state" (p. 1). If one were to accept Page's racial logic and that this was also the motivating force behind Sharpton's campaign, it still does not necessarily follow the devastating consequences Page attributes to this election loss. One would only need to go back to Jackson's victory in South Carolina in the 1980s or Obama's victory in 2008 and 2012 to understand the limits of this analysis. Put simply, winning or losing this state does not determine the success for an African American candidate running for President; Jackson lost the Democratic nomination in 1984 and 1988, and Obama won the Democratic nomination in 2008 and 2012. One could also safely conclude that Jackson's campaign style and political philosophy was most similar to Sharpton's, and Obama's was at the complete polar opposite of this spectrum of African American candidates' style and political philosophy. Arguably the lack of Sharpton's campaign strength in terms of finances, political experience, and staff played a more prominent role in his poor showing in South Carolina. Page goes on to suggest that, "most black voters decided their best bet was Kerry or Edwards," and concludes that "if you define 'black candidates' not by the color of their skin but the color of their supporters, two white men, Kerry and Edwards, appear to have made better black candidates than Sharpton" (p. 1). Page sets up standards of evaluating presidential candidates in terms of national electability and suggests this is the overriding concern of all voters, regardless of race. In making this argument he inadvertently devalues and neglects what might be considered legitimate African American concerns. To be able to illustrate this point, it is important to understand that how Page develops this argument is based on a very common and flawed logic used by the mainstream media that is an established part of our shared political discourse.

On one level, Page's electability argument is very appealing and soothing. One only needs to talk about the previous four years of the Bush presidency to appreciate the anger and disgust many African Americans felt towards this president. Page suggests that, "A lot of black Democrats still feel cheated by the long-count in Florida in 2000, and they are hardly alone." Page then states that, "Many also feel outraged that the Bush presidency turned from a vow of 'compassionate conservatism' to a 'No Child Left Behind' program that appears destined to leave scores of kids behind in schools funded even more poorly than they were before" (p. 1). Based on this reality, clearly a vast number of African Americans were ready for a change and believed that the U.S. could do better than this unmitigated disaster of a presidency. It would not be surprising then that this national mood for many Democrats was reflected in the following comments from Page: "Based on exit polls, the concerns of black voters were pretty much the same that we have heard from other Democrats this season: The issue of electability trumped all others" (p. 1). On another level, one could also certainly question the simple notion that the Democratic with the most "electability" would actually not just defeat Bush but also deliver tangible results to the African American community. It is on this level that Page's use of a condescending and smug tone in his critique of Sharpton ultimately falls flat. This tension in Page's work is most noticeable when he suggests that, "Black voters, like other Democrats, approached this election with a seriousness that the Sharpton candidacy, like that of Kucinich, lacks" (p. 1). To make this point, Page offers the following blistering critique of the Sharpton campaign: "His one-liners are entertaining. So was his little James Brown soft-shoe on 'Saturday Night Live'" (p. 1). Page then seems to undermine his own critiques by suggesting in the next line that, "the stakes of this election are too high, in the view of many black voters, to waste a vote on a smooth-talking pastor who appears to be out to make a point and a name for himself and not much else" (p. 1). Whereas all of these critiques could be considered accurate and valuable critiques of the Sharpton campaign, these critiques do not reinforce or expand upon the points Page previously made about the Bush legacy. In other words, if it was devastating policy positions and legislation that Bush supported that harmed the African American community, then where is the candidate who will not just challenge these areas of the Bush presidency, but substantially move political discourse and public policy into a space that is more friendly and receptive to African American interest? What is the likelihood that the so-called "serious" candidates Page is referencing in this passage will represent African American interest better than the candidates he is dismissing as not serious? Put simply, Page's critique of Sharpton fixates mainly on personal style and delivery of message, not the significant and noticeable policy differences that existed between the Bush presidency and what someone like Sharpton was advocating for and publicly challenging.

Page remains locked in this racial logic for the Sharpton campaign and what his appeal should have been for African American voters. Page starts by making the point that, "Black Americans are not monolithic," and that, "they don't rush to vote for a candidate simply because he or she is black" (p. 1). It is from this vantage point that Page is able to claim that "Rev. Sharpton has discovered" this insight and that, "when any group of people feels put upon as a group, one should not be surprised to see those people respond as a group." (p. 1) What is fascinating is that even if Page was correct in his assessment of electability, then the fact that the Democratic nominee in 2004, Senator John Kerry, still lost to Bush would need to be evaluated. One could make the case that Kerry was not the most electable candidate and that other candidates who ran, such as Senator John Edwards, or even candidates who did not run, such as Senator Hillary Clinton, would have been more "electable" in a race against Bush. With that said, one could still ask if Kerry, Edwards, Clinton, or any other candidate would have made a substantial difference in the areas Page identified as particular concerns for African Americans, such as the No Child Left Behind education policy. It is at this level of argument of what is best for and what is needed for the African American community that Page's argument is not persuasive. This point can be made by simply returning to the previous reference to the Jackson and Obama campaigns. From the vantage point of these two campaigns, it would be very easy to surmise that the Iowa caucus was of much greater significance than the South Carolina primary. What made Obama successful and made him "electable" was his victory in Iowa in 2008, and this was a state that had never elected an African American to a statewide election before. It goes without saying that no other African American presidential candidate had won this state, but the same could not be said about South Carolina. Iowa is positioned as the first caucus and first state to vote in the Democratic Party nomination process. The momentum Obama gained from this victory on one level was short lived since he went on to lose in the next state, New Hampshire, but then, of course, won the third state election in South Carolina, and his campaign gained significant national attention and political power.

This background information in some respects complicates and contradicts some of Page's key points. For starters, one could ask if Obama was the most "electable" candidate or if Clinton or even Edwards would have been more appealing candidate against McCain. Next, one could ask about which candidate best represented African American concerns and issues. Given the policy recorded and legislative agenda of the Obama administration, it is a fair question to raise in terms of how different a policy record and legislative agenda would another candidate have had for the African American communities? Whereas it might be very enjoyable to poke fun at Sharpton and other African American candidates perceived by the mainstream media to be marginal candidates with little to no value in the traditional political realm, it does not necessarily follow that Democratic or Republican presidential candidates and office holders have the best interest of the African American community at heart. Given the simple equation of political success for Democrats on a presidential level, the political party on a national level that typically receives around 80% to 90% of the African American vote has not produced any more or less tangible results for the African American community. It is also not a simple equation that "serious" and "electable" African American candidates are more likely to be supported by White or Black voters, nor will these candidates necessarily have any better developed and more thoughtful public-policy agendas for racial minorities.

It is from this vantage point that Congresswoman Cynthia McKinney's campaign can be reviewed. She also ran in the same 2008 presidential election as Obama, and her stature as a former Democratic member of Congress would have seemed to have offered her a useful platform, but she decided to run as a Green Party candidate. What led her to this decision can be seen in her rocky tenure in Congress that included being defeated twice in Democratic Party primaries for her congressional seat. This history is summarized in the following statement from Waters (2009): "Critics of Cynthia McKinney may dismiss her as a loose cannon and a rabble-rouser, but to her supporters, the former Georgia congresswoman is someone with the courage to challenge convention and speak the truth. McKinney, 54, represented an Atlanta-area district as a Democrat from 1993–2003 and 2005-07" (p. 1). According to Waters, what garnered McKinney the most attention was her critique of U.S. policy toward Israel, and this scathing critique of U.S. foreign policy led to her downfall. Waters presents this argument by first suggesting that, "An advocate of peace and international human rights, she (McKinney) opposed the first Gulf War in 1991 while still a state legislator, and was an early and vocal critic of the Iraq war as well" (p. 1). From this point Waters then claims that, "In Congress, she was a rarity in American politics for her willingness to criticize Israel's treatment of Palestinians," and "along the way, however, she has given off hints that her distaste for Israel's policies contained elements of anti-Semitism—and that has caused her trouble" (p. 1).

Waters concludes this discussion of the rise and fall of McKinney's political career in the following way:

> She was defeated in the 2002 Democratic primary by an opponent who drew financial backing from supporters of Israel and opponents of McKinney's radical statements. The night before the primary, her father, a Georgia state legislator, declared on Atlanta television that "Jews have bought everybody. Jews. J-E-W-S." (p. 1).

Once McKinney was associated with this level of anti-Semitism, her political future was severely damaged. Given her interest in remaining politically active and engaged, it was understandable for her to throw her lot in with the Green Party. At first blush, McKinney's campaign could be considered be even less consequential than the other previously discussed African American candidates. Waters highlights these dynamics of McKinney's campaign by offering the following the insights: "McKinney and the Green Party were on the ballot in 31 states and the District of Columbia. She got just 161,000 votes, slightly more than one-tenth of 1% of the total, and did not affect the outcome of the general election; three other minor-party candidates finished ahead of her" (p. 1). These dismal results do not correspond directly to her actual campaign planks. For example, the way in which McKinney connected environmental policy positions and foreign-policy critiques was well within progressive boundaries, as captured in Sheppard's (2008) work: "'Right now we've got two energy policies in this country,' McKinney told Grist. 'One is war, the other is drilling. And neither one of them works.' It's a message she hopes will win over voters who have tired of both the Democratic and Republican parties" (p. 1). Ultimately McKinney's campaign did not fare any better than those of Gregory, Chisholm, Mosely Braun, or Sharpton. She had a similar political background to Chisholm and arguably political positions not far removed from Sharpton's, but this did not seem to matter. Regardless of the political strengths and resources African American candidates have been able to cobble together, they have not been successful in winning the nomination of one of the two major political parties or the presidency. It is also true that some of the candidates would be considered "protest" candidates, and others would be considered to have been flawed candidates and/or had poorly organized campaigns. What happens when an African American candidate adequately addresses these areas and mounts a campaign that gains national traction? This question presents a more complicated and confusing case study to examine. Jackson's campaign will now be utilized as the case study to address this question. His campaign will be analyzed within the context of the previously discussed African American presidential campaigns as well as the context of what lessons the Obama campaign might have gleaned from Jackson's two presidential bids.

RUN, JESSE, RUN!

Jesse Jackson's 1984 and 1988 campaigns were spectacular political and social events, and the political reverberations of his campaigns can arguably still be felt today. The election of Obama has highlighted this point and brought attention back to Jackson's campaign. Most of the interest that has been generated revolves around the way in which the Jackson and Obama campaigns appear to be appropriate bookends for the trajectory of African American presidential campaigns — two unsuccessful attempts to win the Democratic Party nomination by an African American man in 1984 and 1988 and then two successful bids to win the Democratic Party nomination by another African American man in 2008 and 2012. What is more clear is that the impact of multiple African American presidential campaigns not only influenced Jackson's campaign but arguably can be detected in the way that Obama ran his campaign and the successful path to electoral victory he encountered twice for the Democratic Party nomination and twice for general presidential election victories. At first blush the Jackson campaign represents the civil rights generation, and Jackson was the torch bearer for this generation of activists and organizers. It then makes sense to see his presidential campaign failures as a stepping stone for the future success of a post-civil-rights generation candidate, in particular, the way that Obama's successful presidential campaign can be seen as a direct reaction to the major weaknesses and strengths of Jackson's campaign. This is why the simple representation of Jackson as a very outspoken activist civil rights leader and as a very liberal ideological candidate is contrasted to the way Obama presented himself as a post-racial candidate not rooted in past political struggles, as a consensus builder, and as a moderate Democrat. These two campaigns are highlighted and emphasized at the expense of other African American candidates' campaigns because of the national media attention and the national political legitimacy they were bestowed with. For Jackson and Obama, the way in which their racial identities played prominent roles in their campaigns and the historical legacy of failed African American presidential campaigns weighed heavy on their campaign styles and their public positions on many issues. The problematic dynamic of how racial minorities running for office on a national level must not only build appeal and standing beyond their racial group but also find a way to significantly connect with the dominant race on political as well as stylistic grounds in a way that does not run afoul of the overarching racial tropes was part of the dynamics that plagued both the Jackson and Obama campaign.

Jackson launched his political campaign for the Democratic Party nomination in 1984 from a non-traditional vantage point but still within the boundaries of liberal progressive tradition in the Democratic Party. This can be seen in the analysis of his first formal speech offered by Barker (1989): "I seek the presidency," he said, "to serve notice at a level where I can help restore a moral tone, a redemptive spirit, and sensitivity to the poor and the disposed of the nation" (p. 71). Barker provides the following point about Jackson's speech: "He said he wanted to offer the nation 'a clear choice,' not the vague and centrist politics so strongly supported by the cherished myth and belief that the 'middle way is the best way'" (p. 71). Barker also specifically highlights the way Jackson discussed racism: "He talked about the bitter and divisive racism that still remains and how this must be dealt with directly by the Democratic Party and its candidates." (p. 71) For Jackson, an ordained Baptist minister steeped in the civil rights political philosophy of peace and justice, this opening statement was very fitting. It can also be seen as part of the long tradition of progressive populist candidates who have historically made alliances with the most marginal groups in society. Jackson decided to take this platform to the Democratic Party and not run as a third-party or even an independent candidate. On a certain level his stature as a civil rights leader gave his campaign a very solid foundation. Jackson was already a well-established and respected leader. Jackson even claimed to have been the last person to see Reverend Martin Luther King, Jr. alive and that he was the first one to hold King after he was assassinated (Purnick & Oreskes, 1989). From this vantage point Jackson was able to immerse his campaign in the politics of marginal communities, as well as test the waters of a mainstream campaign.

The way Jackson negotiated these potentially contradictory political commitments, goals, and expectations is worth exploring. On one level

Jackson was not just aware of the fact that he was an African American running for president, but he was also cognizant the weight of the race that he was responsible for carrying. Barker (1989) describes how Jackson drove home this point in the way he summarized his views on why there should be a Black presidential candidate.

> Why run? Blacks have their backs against the wall. They are increasingly distressed by the erosion of past gains and the rapidly deteriorating conditions within black and poor communities. As black leaders have attempted to remedy these problems through the Democratic party — of which black voters have been the most loyal and disciplined followers — too often have they been ignored and treated with disrespect. Mounting a serious presidential candidacy is one way of insisting that black leaders play significant roles and help to shape policy and programs for the party (p. 59).

This statement most succinctly links back to the pioneer campaigns of Gregory and Chisholm, who could be most easily identified as racial trailblazers in this respect. These sentiments could also be seen in the Sharpton and McKinney campaigns. Past and future African American presidential candidates would no doubt agree with and appreciate the shared racial weight of oppression and the lack of political attention and commitment from both of the major political parties. To the extent that an African American candidate can become pigeonholed into being a "Black" or a "race" candidate, then that would immediately place him/her in the fringe category.

Given the lack of actual political voting strength for the African American community, candidates have no possibility of winning a national election without appeal to the dominant White race. Jackson attempted to maneuver out of this self-imposed box, as can be seen in the way Walters (1999) describes his attempt to create a broad coalition of support:

"In addition, Rev. Jackson was adamant that it would not be only a black campaign, so an important collection of the leadership of white progressive women, youth, gay, and other issue-oriented originations, combined with some of the leaders of 'third world' minorities such as native Americans, Hispanics, Arabs, Asians, and others, were attracted to the support of his campaign" (p. 37). Walters also draws attention to the reality that, "Although this grouping became known as the 'Rainbow Coalition,' support had not materialized from the main-line leaders of these groups nor from any major white politicians or establishment institutional leaders" (p. 37). The appeal of Jackson's campaign was noticeable, and his approach was relatively successful, but ultimately one could conclude that this effort was doomed for failure. His failure was not just in terms of his inability to win the Democratic Party presidential nomination but also from the standpoint of potential damage done to African American involvement and engagement in presidential politics and campaigns.

One way to appreciate the dilemma that Jackson faced is to examine the way the dual dilemma of being labeled a "Black" candidate while also attempting to be considered a mainstream electable and viable candidate. In fact, placed in the context of his second-place finish in the race for the Democratic Party nomination for president, the following analysis from Purnick and Oreskes (1987) provides a persuasive argument for how these dynamics operated in the Jackson campaign: "Jesse Jackson could arrive at the Democratic National Convention in Atlanta next July with more delegates than any other candidate," and "Most political analysts give him little chance of being nominated—partly because he is black, partly because of his unretrenched liberalism" (p. 121). From this vantage point Purnick and Oreskes suggest that, "While he argues that he would be accepted as the front-runner if he were white, it is also possible that his race gives him an edge—that his politics, personal flamboyance, and campaign flaws would long since have forced another candidate out of the race" (p. 121). What is most striking about this analysis of the Jackson campaign is the ease with which Black concerns and liberalism are presented as interchangeable and manageable parts. The underlying assumption seems to be that if Jackson could just drop the liberalism part or the Black part of his campaign, he could be a top-tier candidate. The fact that the "liberalism" Jackson espouses is inextricably linked to his Black racial identity appears to be completely lost in this analysis. Purnick and Oreskes suggest that, "Of the six declared Democratic presidential candidates, Jesse Jackson is the most unabashed advocate of increased government spending for social programs, from farm subsidies to housing" (p. 27). Jackson's position was not formed out of thin air, nor was it done to simply position himself as the most "Black" or "liberal" candidate. What motivated and propelled Jackson's 1984 and 1988 campaigns were the actual conditions on the ground for millions of racial minorities during the Reagan presidency. This point is highlighted by Barker's (1989) work: "Specifically, the Reagan administration illuminated vividly how the actions of a president can directly affect our everyday lives" (p. 9). Barker then goes on to suggest that, "Budget cuts and budget allocation indicated clearly that the interests of blacks, women, minorities, and the poor were not among the priority interest of the Reagan administration," and "This was exemplified in the administration's stance toward certain social benefit programs, legal aid services, and the implementation and enforcement of civil rights laws in general" (p. 9). One could take away from these insights that not only was a Jackson campaign needed, but that it was reasonable for any Democratic Party candidate to faithfully and sincerely address these issues. The fact that the two White men who won the Democratic party nomination in 1984 (Mondale) and 1988 (Dukakis) not only lost the presidential elections but also arguably would have done very little to address many of the areas of harm and damage to racial-minority communities that the Reagan presidency had intensified suggests that the labels and terms used to explain the Jackson campaign are inadequate. To suggest that an African American candidate attempting to raise these issues and give them prominence in his/her candidacy would be too "Black" or too "liberal" highlights the dual dilemma all African American presidential candidates have encountered.

The lingering dual burden of race and liberalism that the Jackson campaign encountered remained firmly in place for future African American candidates. Jackson represented the most significant advancement for an

African American candidate vying for a major-party nomination, as well as the highest level of electoral success any racial-minority candidate had received. Sharpton, Mosley Braun, and McKinney did not advance beyond Jackson's level of success, and their campaigns arguably had no electoral impact and very little impact beyond the very narrow circle of supporters these campaigns had to start with. Obama's campaign clearly was the one that succeeded and the one that adroitly maneuvered through these previously covered hurdles. At least two potential readings of Jackson's campaign could be gleaned from his success and his failure. One sympathetic reading could focus on his electoral success and suggest it is possible to adequately address the previously mentioned dual dilemmas of race and liberalism. Specifically, it could be noted that in 1984 Jesse Jackson received 3,282,431 votes or 18.09% of the Democratic primary vote. He finished in third place (out of the five major candidates), and he won primaries and caucuses in Louisiana, the District of Columbia, South Carolina, and Mississippi. In 1988 Jackson produced even more tangible electoral results: Jackson's vote total was 6,788,991 or 29.13%. He also came in second place behind Dukakis, and he beat out six other major Democratic Party candidates in this election cycle. Jackson was victorious in eleven primaries and caucuses including Alabama, the District of Columbia, Georgia, Louisiana, Mississippi, Puerto Rico, Virginia, Delaware, Michigan, South Carolina, and Vermont. From this vantage point, Jackson's campaign looks substantially more viable and significant than all of the previous African American candidates' campaigns for presidency, and his campaign moved solidly into the realm of mainstream and relevant campaigns. Based on this reading of his campaign, one could argue that Jackson was not far from winning the Democratic nomination and that his campaign might have only needed some minor alternations in campaign strategy and tactics. Put simply, it might not have been the impossibly of his "Blackness" or his "liberalism" that doomed his campaign, but areas such as inadequate fund raising, state campaign strategy, and candidate verbal gaffes that presented the greatest hurdle for his campaign. One could also add to this reading of the Jackson campaign that the fact he did have this level of electoral success and was considered to be a mainstream candidate brought his campaign message to millions of people who might not have ever been exposed to this type of political message. In particular, one could emphasize the way in which Jackson attempted to connect to the African American community and how unique this approach was within the standard frame of national campaigns and political discourse.

Blacks receive more of the "symbols" than the substance of politics, while whites have both in relative abundance. The purpose of Jackson's campaign was to change this situation. Through his charisma and oratorical skills, Jackson stood to provide the sort of symbolic focus and appeal that could stir the interest and attention of those who had been outside the political process or who had remained relatively politically inactive. Getting attention in political campaigns is indispensable. A Jackson candidacy could provide a symbolic focus that would activate people who then would proceed to vote their substantive interests (Barker, 1989).

Based on the description of the Jackson campaign that Barker provides, one could apply the logic of this approach to other disadvantaged communities, and one could make the case that this was the most unique feature of the Jackson campaign. "What made the Jackson campaign new and distinct to American voters was not simply or even primarily his racial identity nor the fact that he had never held political office, but most especially that he sought to mobilize the support of the historically disposed, a 'rainbow coalition' of blacks, Hispanics, women, young people, lower-income whites, and activists form various liberal causes. Historically most of these groups have voted at far lower rates than marginal voter-groups far more difficult to mobilize in large numbers" (Barker, 1989, p. 35). The potential long-term ripple effect of Jackson's campaign would be to increase the political activism and consciousness in marginal political communities. The impact of this strategy would not be easy to identify within the context of simple electoral gains, nor would these results be seen in just one or two election cycles. This analysis could be extended to look at how far Jackson might have moved the Democratic Party to the "left" of the political spectrum and what specific planks in the party platform Jackson could have influenced. It could also include the amount of Jackson's delegates that went to the Democratic Party convention and what role these delegates played in the conventional. All of this suggests a much more complicated and nuanced analysis of Jackson's campaign is needed and that his campaigns can be evaluated in a myriad of ways. This sympathetic reading provides a significant counterpoint to the deeply critical mainstream reading of Jackson's campaign.

It is now important to evaluate the critical readings of Jackson's campaign and to understand why this has become the dominant narrative for his campaign. An example of this critique can be seen in the work of Lorenzo Morris and Linda F. Williams (1989): "For all its originality and all of Jackson's magnificent eloquence and dramatic flair, the Jackson campaign was mostly significant for its lack of influence on the outcome" (p. 57). As suggested by Morris and Williams, this emphasis on Jackson's electoral defeat could lead to a particular reading that would question whether or not an African American running for president carries too great a risk for racial minorities: "The Jackson candidacy may have actually re-legitimatized the American electoral system to such an extent that blacks will simply accept that they were beaten and a conservative agenda won fairly" and the specific point that, "Increasingly, blacks, especially middle-class blacks who vote most often, might feel that it is time jump on the political bandwagon of conservatism to secure at least individualistic gains" (p. 58). The logic that informs this analysis of Jackson's 1984 campaign is based on connecting the harm and damage inflicted on communities of color during the Reagan Administration to the realistic expectations placed upon African American presidential candidates. If the expectation is that African American candidates will be fierce advocates for their racial communities and that this advocacy will appear to be liberal, then it will never be possible for an African American candidate for president to win a presidential election — at least not through the Democratic Party.

One could even go so far as to propose the following idealist sentiment from Barker (1989) for evaluating African American presidential candidates: "Thus, as it developed, the strategy of a black presidential candidacy threatened some very fundamental aspects of our basic social and belief structure (symbols, mechanism, processes, myths, etc.) which undergirds much of our politics and public policies" (p. 16). To the extent that this was true, then the points that Barker makes should follow: "It would certainly focus attention on the structures and processes by which influence and benefits are distributed" (p. 16). Even more concretely, Barker claims that, "A serious black presidential candidacy would concretely challenge all Americans to consider what they fear, what they regard as possible, and even who they are" (p. 16). To the extent then that this analytical frame can be applied to the Jackson campaign, then it can be understood why the dual dilemma of race and liberalism became an insurmountable hurdle for him to negotiate through and succeed politically. It is based on this backdrop of Jackson's failure and the degree of difficulty facing his presidential campaigns that one concludes that an African American would never be able to win the presidency. From the vantage point of Obama's presidential campaign victories in 2008 and 2012, we know that this is not true. This returns us to the fundamental question of how and why Obama was so successful in this area when so many other African Americans before him failed. What did Obama do that was different from previous African American candidates, and how was he successful? To be able to address these questions in the next section, the significance and potency of race and racism in presidential elections will be examined.

SAMPLE OF THE RACIST ATTACKS

For all of the aspersions cast on negative campaigning and despite the many ailments of the body politic attributed to it, many a scholar has acknowledged its valuable contribution to free elections.

Buell, Jr. and Sigelman, 2008.

INTRODUCTION

The way in which race and racism has been interjected in subtle and overt forms on previous presidential campaigns and presidential tenure in office suggests that its impact is much greater than the simple racial identity of a particular candidate or even his/her stance on specific policy issues. This historical analysis offers invaluable insights into the all-encompassing way race has seeped into every aspect of presidential campaigns and presidential administrations' governing style and legislative agenda. When a specific examination of the African Americans that have run for president is launched some unmistakable themes arise. One is the fact that until Obama won the presidency in 2008 none of the previous campaigns had been successful. In fact, Obama was the first racial minority to win the nomination of a major political party. The corollary for this failure is usually tightly tied to a racial logic, and the emphasis is placed on the candidates' racial identity. This suggests that what stands out most for these candidates is not necessarily their campaign platforms, organizational style, or even political experience. The previous section highlighted the substantial and subtle differences between many of the African American candidates that have run for president and suggests that it was simply their racial identity that led to their campaign demise. Where race began to play a prominent role was in documenting and interpreting the electoral success the Jackson campaign encountered in 1984 and 1988. This success was markedly different from other African American candidates, but the way Jackson embraced his racial identity and constructed his political platform out of this political identity was very similar to the strategy used by what had been considered even the most marginal African American candidates.

This then set the stage for the Obama campaign and how it would maneuver through these same formidable barriers as the Jackson campaign and all of the other previous African American candidates. What makes the Obama campaign stand out in this respect is the fact that he positioned himself and marketed himself in the complete opposite direction of the Jackson campaign. Unlike the qualms and difficulties other African American candidates had gone through in terms of developing a political platform that was in tune with their racial identity and how they might want to carry the weight of their race, Obama openly disavowed this racial logic and plotted a political course that was race neutral. Obama's national introduction to politics, and for many his most memorable, remains his 2004 Democratic Party keynote speech.

In his speech Obama not only riffs off of the false distinctions made between Blue (Democratic) and Red (Republican) states, but how all barriers, racial and non-racial, should, and cannot, divide us:

> There's not a black America and white America and Latino America and Asian America; there's the United States of America. The pundits, the pundits

like to slice and dice our country into red states and blue states: red states for Republicans, blue states for Democrats. But I've got news for them, too. We worship an awesome God in the blue states, and we don't like federal agents poking around our libraries in the red states. We coach Little League in the blue states and, yes, we've got some gay friends in the red states. (Obama, 2004)

This literally built and established his political brand, and to this day his speech still represents the political image Obama proudly projects. His message was perfectly tailored for a "post-racial" generation of voters, and he became the embodiment of racial healing and racial reconciliation. This political presentation of an African American candidate for president was radically different than the way Jackson built his political brand.

Jackson's political presentation and foundation was rooted in the more customary tradition of identity politics. Jackson made this argument in the following way:

"This candidacy is not for black only. This is a national campaign growing out of the black experience and seen through the eyes of the black perspective—which is the experience and perspective of the reject-ed. Because of this experience, I can empathize with the plight of the Appalachia because I have known poverty. I know the pain of anti-Semitism because I have felt the humiliation of discrimination. I know first-hand the shame of breadlines and the horror of hopelessness and despair because my life has been dedicated to empowering the world's rejected to be-come respected. Thus, our perspective encompasses and includes more of the American people and their respective interests than do most other experiences" (Morris & Williams, 1989, p. 13).

It could be assumed by virtue of Obama's success that he made the correct choice and that his path was the one that was needed and demanded of an African American candidate. As previously covered with the Jackson campaign the constant drumbeat of attacks on his liberal politics and his perceived poor racial treatment made it extremely difficult for his campaign to gain any national momentum or broad appeal. Obama's campaign would seem to follow the implied logic of the mainstream critiques of the Jackson campaign from twenty years earlier, and Obama's campaign then created the political brand and structure to move well beyond Jackson's success. Based on the assumed logic of this premise being accurate, what became the most striking aspect of the Obama campaign was not the lack of the nagging racial conundrums and obstacles that previous African American candidates experienced but rather the extraordinary amount and intensity of the racial attacks Obama encountered that made race and racism a central feature of his campaign. The argument that can be advanced now is that even the most careful and concerted effort by an African American presidential candidate to conceal and downplay his racial identity, as well as any connection this identity might have to his public positions and legislative agenda, was also doomed to fail. What follows would be a need to take into account not only the simple electoral success associated with Obama as the first African American president but also the larger racial discourse that has had an impact on previous African American candidates for president, as well as other presidential candidates and office holders. Whereas it might be true that a critical component of Obama's successful campaign branding and strategy was based on "post-racial" political branding, it is also the case that the level of intensity and the sheer number of racial attacks that were directed at Obama were not unlike those any other previous African American presidential candidate had encountered. From this backdrop, the uniqueness of the Obama campaign can be examined as well as a way to constructively guage his successful presidential campaigns, as well as his time in office.

This provides a context from which Obama's 2008 presidential election can be critically analyzed. It is now possible to make the case for not only the negative campaign Obama encountered being substantially different than what has been suggested by historical precedent but that a great deal of this negative campaigning was also of a racist nature. To be able to substantiate the racial nature of this campaign and the devastating long-term impact of these attacks, it is important to first define and explain the way in which race will be used in this work and then, second, offer concrete examples of how the negative campaign Obama faced included subtle and overt racist messages. Through this analytical process, the weaknesses and limitations of the previous scholarship on negative presidential campaigning will be critically reviewed. This will then set the stage for why the 2008 Democratic primary and general election can be described as inflicting a form of "racial trauma" on racial minorities. This most recent trauma is still reverberating through the social, political, and economic environment. This analysis will be offered as a framework for examining the experience of the first African American president as he successfully navigated his way through the primary and general elections before becoming president, as well as during his tenure as president.

There are numerous definitions of race and racism, and there is a great deal of debate about these definitions. The way race and racism will be used in this book relies heavily upon social scientific scholarship and insights. In particular, an emphasis will be placed on the way race and racism are socially constructed and how this social construction process relies on a hierarchal system based on European superiority and non-European inferiority. Historically race was used as a way to measure perceived phenotypical differences, and this scientific pursuit contributed to the building of a faulty "race-based" biological understanding of human beings. Through an examination of multiple texts, I will elaborate on how race and racism continue to operate as a socially constructed phenomenon and how power relations continue to provide the basis of the way race relations continue to function. To highlight these key points, I will start with Lynn Webber's work on the larger matrix of identity politics. In her book, *Understanding Race, Class, Gender, and Sexuality: A Conceptual Framework*, she argues that race is inextricably linked to other forms of oppressive identity and that these other forms of identity need to be incorporated into any race-based analysis. The next text that I will examine is Michael Omi and Howard Winant's book, *Racial Formation in the United States: From the 1960s to the 1980s*. This text presents a more formal approach that many social scientists have utilized for the study of race and racism. The last text is Joe Feagin's book, *Racist America: Roots, Current Realities, and Future Reparations* which illuminates an understanding of race and racism not just from the primary axis of Black and White relations, but also from the standpoint of how entrenched and fundamental race is for contemporary, as well as historical, American society.

The other key element of these attacks is not just how insidious and destructive they were in terms of the racial messages utilized, but because of the racial nature of these attacks, very few viable options were available to then-candidate Obama to respond. On one hand, to respond to these attacks, Obama by declaring them and/or the perpetrators of these attacks as racist would have run the risk of a severe White backlash that could have included Obama being labeled an angry Black man who was willing to play the "race card" in response to any political attack. On the other hand, Obama could choose to not respond by ignoring the attack (and the racist nature of the attack), and this would provide him with the opportunity to avoid being pigeonholed as the "racialized" Black candidate. Obama clearly made the crude political calculation to offer no response to these attacks, and certainly there was not a concerted effort by Obama, the Democratic Party, or any of his "official" surrogates to draw attention to the racial nature of any of the attacks he received during or after the elections in 2008. Much of what has been written about the Obama presidency has assumed that the first Black president would encounter novel attacks and that some of these attacks might even be based on subtle or overt racism. Very little attention has been given to how these attacks and his response to these attacks would define his time in office.

To the extent that Obama was accepted and understood as a "Black" president and not an "American" president, he would run the risk of being marginalized on a national stage. To the extent that Obama could be understood and defined in terms of Black historical figures and events, it was critical that Obama, through his campaign, could gain control over this narrative. The work of Tim Wise will be used to elaborate on this point and to highlight the significance of how this racial framing worked for Obama. Once placed in this racial context, Obama's lack of response to the racial assault will begin to make more sense, and the racist attacks could be understood more clearly as an effort to "Blacken" him up. The danger of a stereotypical image of an uppity, belligerent Black man was part of the overt political calculation Obama made to not respond to informal or formal racist negative attacks from his opponents. The possibility of becoming bogged down in the racial accusations and defenses with another White political candidate was too high of a political risk for Obama. One could also submit that Obama's temperament and personality were more in tune with taking a "high road" approach to personal and political attacks, which was the foundation of his approach to attacks. Even with Obama's very well received speech on race given in Philadelphia during the Democratic primary in 2008, Obama clearly did not want to get into the "weeds" of explaining or defending racial accusations with regards to the mainstream media coverage of Reverend Wright. The most profound and engaging part of Obama's speech worked on the level of presenting an American narrative that tilted toward racial progress and uplift. The juxtaposition of this analysis alongside one that views Obama as simply another occupant of the White House who would encounter similar turmoil and obstacles as previous occupants of the White House has rarely been attempted.

WHAT CONSTITUTES RACE AND RACISM?

One way to understand race is to offer a definition within the context of other forms of oppression. In particular, gender and sexuality are also forms of oppression that have been historically constructed and that are also based on a hierarchal power structure. An analysis that incorporates multiple forms of oppression is often referred to as identity politics, and it is the focal point of Weber's work (Weber, 2001). Within Weber's work, the significance of race is not only established, but also the larger frame of identity politics is presented. Weber makes this point by stating, "Race, class, gender, and sexuality are powerful social systems that have structured individual private lives and collective social existence for the entire history of the United States" (p. 3). Weber describes these social relations by placing an emphasis on material exploitation and power relations by declaring that, "race, class, gender, and sexuality are systems of oppression" (p. 1). According to Weber, these oppressive relations can be examined from a historical standpoint: "Oppression exists when one group has historically gained power and control over socially valued assets by exploiting the labor and lives of other groups and using those assets to secure its position of power into the future" (p. 2). This oppression is a critical component of our contemporary lives, and it has a long historical legacy in the U.S. Based on this reading of U.S. history, Weber offers the following analysis of power relations: "In this country, founded on the ideal that 'all men are created equal,' power and privilege, in fact, are distributed not only along individual but also along group lines so that some groups are privileged —Whites, heterosexuals, upper classes, men—while others are oppressed —people of color, gays, bisexuals, lesbians, the working classes, the poor, and women" (p. 4). This understanding of race provides the basis for examining the current racial assaults that have been leveled at President Obama. Based on Weber's presentation of race, class, gender, and sexuality, specific questions about the racial attacks on Obama can be probed: In particular, one could begin to use Weber's analysis to distinguish attacks on previous presidents from the attacks on Obama. In particular, given the similarity of the social standing of the vast majority of presidents (White, male, heterosexual, wealthy, middle aged, Christian), what does it mean to have a president with one social location mark (Black race) significantly outside this terrain? Is Obama's racial identity so significant that in and of itself it is able to elicit so much attention and negative reaction? One could also turn to this specific racial identity and examine what implications this identity has for the larger racial discourse matrix. In particular, one could ask: Do these attacks support an oppressive racial discourse? Broader questions about interlocking forms of oppression could also be addressed. Since Secretary of State Hillary Rodham Clinton was Obama's primary opponent in the Democratic Party primary, it is also relevant to ask if the path Obama has blazed is making it more likely or less likely for minorities from oppressed communities to obtain power at the presidential level and successfully retain this position. Have the constant racial attacks on the president made it easier for future inhabitants of the White House to be someone outside of the traditional social location for this position or has his experience in the White House suggested that the American public is less inclined to support someone from an oppressed minority community obtaining this level of power?

Omi and Winant's (1996) work on race has not only provided social scientists with a foundational text, but, arguably, has provided many significant insights into how the U.S. racial discourse operates. Unlike Weber's work, their analysis is more narrowly focused on race as one system of oppression that operates in the U.S. and the unique character of this racial discourse. One of the key points of Omi and Winant's work is that, "Race will always be at the center of the American experience" (p. 21). They provide a very convincing case for the persistence of an oppressive racial discourse even as it appears to become more benign and less significant. Omi and Winant challenged other scholarly work where, "race is not regarded as a continually evolving category in its own right; in fact, these approaches have often imagined that race would decline in importance, even disappear, as economic or political 'progress' rendered 'race thinking' obsolete" (p. 25). Omi and Winant correctly anticipated the current post-racial debate that has resurfaced in the aftermath of Obama's two elections. In the following passage, Omi and Winant provide a potent counter-narrative to what is now becoming the dominant post-racial outlook of Americans.

> The continuing persistence of racial ideology suggests that these racial myths and stereotypes cannot be exposed as such in the popular imagination. They are, we think, too essential, too integral, to the maintenance of the U.S. social order. Of course, particular meanings, stereotypes and myths can change, but the presence of a system of racial meanings and stereotypes, of racial ideology, seems to be a permanent feature of the U.S. culture (p. 57).

This analysis provides the platform from which the racial assaults leveled at Obama can be critically reviewed, and another series of questions can be presented now: How predicable were the overt and subtle racial attacks on President Obama? What do the popularity and the effectiveness of these attacks reveal about the current state of race relations? Is it possible to "win" race-based political election battles and "lose" larger race-discourse wars? Placed in a historical frame, do these racial attacks on President Obama provide another obstacle for race progress and/or post-racial narratives?

In Joe Feagin's text *Racist America*, the primary prism of viewing race relations from the perspective of a Black and White axis is utilized to present a similar case to Omi and Winant. What also emerges from Feagin's work is a more comprehensive and persuasive argument about the centrality of race in America, and this argument also echoes many of the central tenants of Weber, as well as Omi and Winant's work. An example can be seen in his discussion of how systemic racism historically became engrained in every facet of American life. Feagin starts this discussion with the simple observation that in 1787 fifty- five men gathered in Philadelphia "to write a constitution for what will be called 'the first democratic nation.'" (Feagin, 2001).

He then moves on to describe the exact background of these men:

> Significantly, at least 40 percent have been or are slave owners, and a significant proportion of the others profit to some degree as merchants, shippers, lawyers, and bankers from the trade in slaves, commerce in slave-produced agricultural products, or supplying provisions to slaveholders and slave traders. Moreover, the man who pressed hard for this convention and now chairs it, George Washington, is one of the richest men in the colonies because of hundreds of black men, women, and children he has held in bondage. Washington and his colleagues created the first democratic nation, yet one for whites only. In the preamble to their bold document, the founders cite prominently

"We the People," but this phrase does not encompass
the fifth of the population that is enslaved (p. 38).

These are not novel insights in this well documented history. What is less
explored and understood is how this overt level of racial organizing and
formation at the time of the founding of the country continues to impact
the current political climate.

It can be argued that based on this level of racial analysis, key points
can be gleaned about the racial predicament Obama and the nation found
themselves in. For example, the fact that an opposition party, the Tea
Party, was formed within days after the first Black president was sworn in
and that this new party's most explicit demand seemed to be a "return" to
Constitutional roots, and the fact that this understating of Constitutional
roots relied on a belief that this time period provided the "golden years"
for the United States provides ample support for why the racial analysis
of this historical period that Feagin offers is so poignant. The period that
the Tea Party is most infatuated with, and loyal to, is the period when
African Americans (and Native Americans) had the fewest political rights
and were subjected to the most brutal forms of oppression. The fact that
this fundamental tension is not part of a mainstream discussion about the
Tea Party and also not included in the discussion of the racial attacks on
President Obama reinforces many of Feagin's central tenets.

Feagin claims that on the one hand:

> ..the dominant social science paradigm, seen in much mainstream
> scholarship on 'race,' still views racism as something tacked
> onto an otherwise healthy American society," while on the other
> hand, "the central problem is that from the beginning European-
> American institutions were racially hierarchical, white supremacist
> and undemocratic… [and] they remain so today (p. 3).

From this vantage point, Feagin's work can be understood to anticipate many
of the attacks that President Obama encountered. In particular, the popularity
and the effectiveness of the attacks on Obama's national origin, religion, and

patriotism can be seen as part of a larger racial matrix. Questions arise, such as, were there literally no other attacks that could be imagined or utilized for a Black man running for president, except for ones that had an overt or subtle racial overtone to them? To what extent were these attacks accidental and random, or were they more of a reflection of a calculated assessment of what would be the most effective political attacks on President Obama?

These texts provide the groundwork for not only the meaning and significance of race in our society but also how it continues to operate on a daily basis for our political structures. The ways in which racial ideologies are developed today reflect in the political choices one makes, as well as a person's views of particular politicians. From this backdrop the myriad of attacks on President Obama before and after the 2008 presidential election becomes intelligible. The next section of this book will provide the material evidence of the attacks, and these attacks can then be linked to specific historical and contemporary racist practices and beliefs.

EXAMPLES OF RACIST ATTACKS ON PRESIDENT OBAMA

The work of Weber, Omi, Winant, Dill, and Feagin provide the basis for understanding the selection and use of the racial attacks leveled at Obama and the criteria by which these attacks can be distinguished from other forms of insults and jokes that Obama encountered. These attacks have either overtly mocked or challenged his Black racial identity, or they have subtly attacked his racial identity by probing into the following areas: Birth certificate, the wearing of a flag lapel pin, his church and pastor, his birth name, his religious faith, and his relationship with a former member of the Weather Underground Organization. This is not an exhaustive list of all of the types of attacks that have been leveled at President Obama's life and political career, but these attacks provide an adequate sample of the types of attacks that he encountered since his first presidential run.

A few of the most prominent and significant overt and subtle racial attacks that President Obama confronted since he launched his first presidential campaign in 2007 will be reviewed in this section. These attacks help to shed light on the following questions: Is there a new standard for negative campaigning in presidential elections? Is there a new standard for attacks leveled on at a sitting president? Has the election of Obama and his presidency helped to raise or lower the bar for acceptable racial etiquette? Can racial progress or regression be documented and explained? Depending on how one understands the racial significance of these attacks and the political effectiveness and the social consequences of these attacks, then these attacks could also be considered a new low for American politics.

A presentation of the some of the racial attacks that were directed at President Obama when he was a candidate in 2007 and 2008, and then when he was elected president in 2008 (and started formally serving as president in 2009) can be examined from the vantage point of Weber, Feagin, Omi, and Winant's work on race, as well as Buell, Jr. and Sigelman's work on negative campaigning. The sample of the racial attacks leveled at Obama that are utilized in this section can be placed in one of the following two racial categories:

1   Overt Racism

2   Subtle Racism

In the category of Overt Racism only attacks that have a clear race-based referential point will be examined, whereas in the category of Subtle Racism, more abstract and nuanced racial attacks will be analyzed. All of these attacks can be understood in the larger oppressive identity politics matrix Weber describes, as well as the more limited raced-based oppression that Feagin, Omi and Winant analyze. These attacks can also be placed in the specific context of Obama being the only African American candidate in the 2008 Democratic primary and the general election and how the other front-runner White candidates engaged with and interacted with him during the campaigns.

OVERT RACISM

There were numerous examples of racism manifested during the 2008 Democratic Primary and General Election of 2008. The examples of Overt Racial attacks provide the most easily identifiable racial attacks and the most clear racialized moments of the campaign. There are just five examples that are presented in this section, but there are numerous others that could have been included in this category of Overt Racism.

1. RACIST BUTTONS SOLD BY REPUBLICANS AT A TEXAS STATE CONVENTION

On June 19, 2008, a vendor at a Texas Republican Party convention decided to sell pins that stated: "If Obama is president, will we still call it the White House?" This button represents a racial discourse at a crude and rudimentary level: a Black man in the White House is incomprehensible. This button would not make sense for a White candidate running for president, and the shared American understanding of the meaning of this button is overtly racist. In fact, one

Fig. 4.1.

could easily point out that this button even harkens back to the film *Birth of a Nation* and post-reconstruction time. *Birth of a Nation* presented overtly racist images of African American legislators eating food, putting their feet on desks, and engaging in visibly inappropriate and unacceptable behavior while on the floor of the Capitol. These images represented the fears of Southern Whites during the Reconstruction period about what African Americans right to vote and run for office would result in for the country. The same exaggerated fear of African Americans in political office and what they would do with this power is as critical to one's understanding of *Birth of a Nation* at the beginning of the 20th Century, as it is to understanding this button in 2008. It is also critical to note that what made the selling of this button significant was not simply the fact it was the act of one individual, but the fact that one of the two major political parties played a role in it. This button was being marketed at a state Republican Party Convention, and clearly the vendor distributing this button thought there would be a receptive audience for this message.

2. OBAMA PORTRAYED AS CURIOUS GEORGE ON T-SHIRTS

Fig 4.2.

On May 15, 2008, a bar owner named Mike Norman in Marietta, Georgia, sold t-shirts with a picture of Curious George peeling a banana and the caption "Obama in 08" displayed prominently underneath the image.

This overt racial attack on President Obama relied on the well established racial imagery of Black people as monkeys (sub-human). The novelty of the attack on a candidate running for president is striking. This immediate use of Curious George to represent candidate Obama suggested that not much thought beyond the long history of animals in general, and apes and monkeys in particular, to represent Black men was needed to attack a prominent Black man running for president. There is no meaningful or tangible connection between Obama's particular position on political issues and the use of Curious George. The more common practice of ridiculing and mocking a politician's particular political views or even personal traits takes a back seat to the politically expedient challenge of racial identity and the rich racial discourse this challenging of one's identity can open up.

3. "FAKE" OBAMA MONEY PULLED FROM GOP FAIR BOOTH

Fig. 4.3.

On August 27, 2008, the Snohomish County Republican Party sold "$3 bills" that included Barack Obama wearing Arab headgear with a camel on the back of the bill. This was done at the Evergreen State Fair in Monroe, Washington. The practice of placing Obama's image on fake money became very popular early in the campaign. (This practice appears to be in direct reaction to Obama's proclamation that his image is not seen on money. He was using this comment as a clever way to make the point that Black men running for president are a rarity and that there had not been a Black president.) All of this was done to create a certain tension and stir emotions. In particular, the practice not only included adding Obama's image to money, but his image was always created with overtly racist symbols and messages. The fact that the "$3 bills" used at the Snohomish County Republican Party event utilized Arab and Muslim images does not simply reflect upon Obama's Muslim father and questions about his own religious faith, but also displays how easily these symbols could be digested as new racial assaults. Since the 9/11 tragedy, Muslim and Arab imagery and symbols have become a symbolic shorthand for America's enemies and the most despised religion/people. Placing this package on a Black man running for president added the element of not only the racial identity of the candidate (Black), but the current racial hatred of a group and religion (Arabs/Muslims). The political currency used to attack Obama relied upon his father's racial identity and religion and completely disregarded political positions (such as his stance on the war on terrorism) or even his mother's identity (White, Midwestern, female, and Christian). Race not only became easy "target" for Obama's detractors, but it literally sucked all the other political oxygen out of the room.

4. RACIST IMAGES OF OBAMA PUT ON WAFFLE BOXES

On September 13, 2008, a vendor was selling "Obama Waffles" at a Values Voter Summit, and, as in the previous examples, this was described as innocent and/or a simple mistake. Obama's image on a waffle box immediately brings to mind Aunt Jemima. The use of a slave woman to sell maple syrup

Fig 4.4.

and other products has been a staple of marketing for decades. The fact that "Obama Waffles" would be presented in this fashion is not surprising when placed in the context of the historical use of Black caricatures to sell products. Aunt Jemima represents a seal of authenticity for the makers of syrup and in the marketplace of ideas and symbols, and the producers of this product gambled that this image would be more appealing than other images. It is not hard to imagine that this same calculation was made by the makers of "Obama Waffles." Even a prominent conservative pundit who used to have a popular weeknight television news show on CNN, Lou

Dobbs, was interested in purchasing this product for his wife and seemed to have no qualms about the racist imagery used to display this product. This product was not, then, based on an isolated decision by someone to sell a product with overtly racist imagery but part of a larger racialized structural setting where this product was given a venue (Values Voter Summit) and a receptive audience for its racist message (product popular with noteworthy conservative political figures and television host).

5. MORE RACIST "OBAMA BUCKS"

Fig. 4.5. California Republican women's group sent out a newsletter showing this fake $10 "food stamp."

A California Republican women's group sent out a newsletter showing this fake $10 "food stamp" with Obama's face and stereotypical racist imagery included on it. In another example of "Obama Bucks," the racial imagery rings true and proudly. This time it is a fake $10 bill made to look like a "legitimate" food stamp. The use of a food stamp relies on a shared understanding of Black people being poor, lazy, and more than likely to be on welfare. It also prominently displays symbols to connote a stupid and pitiful Black race: A bucket of Kentucky Fried Chicken, ribs, Kool Aid, and watermelon. The novelty of placing a presidential candidate in this camp directly connects to a racial narrative that was being promoted and supported by many people.

All of these items, from the chicken to the Kool Aid to watermelon, have a long historical significance of being used in a discriminatory fashion against African Americans and were clearly not selected on a random basis or based on Obama's personal tastes and preferences. These items selected did not represent public policy decisions or positions either. For example, Obama had no specific public policy positions about government assistance programs for poor people that prompted this image or any discernible political positions in general that were being attacked. The fact that Obama is Black appears to be the only license needed to justify and successfully place his image on a "food-stamp bill." The presentation of Obama in a donkey outfit does not just associate him with a political party but also adds to this sub-human sentiment. This provides another fundamental questioning of Obama's humanity, and this image relies heavily upon a history of Blacks being presented as non- or sub-human.

Even though this is a select group of images and they have some significant differences in their presentations of Obama, when these presentations are examined in their totality, vital themes begin to emerge. Some of the critical themes in these racial attacks include the number of attacks (not one isolated incident), the novelty of the attacks (the racial identity of a major presidential candidate has never been called into question in such a manner); institutional and organizational support (Republican Party and conservative activist functions and established businesses/venues utilized), historical legacy (direct connection to past racial images and symbols), and marketability and popularity (audience interest and susceptibility to this material). These themes are also invaluable for understanding the attacks that fall into the Subtle Racism category, and these are the themes that will be developed in the next section.

SUBTLE RACISM

In the category of Subtle Racism, the following sub-groupings could be offered: Citizenship, Patriotism, Religious Faith, and Birth Name. All of these attacks have an element of normal political discourse, but they are also firmly embedded in a discourse of race and racism. The way in which this operates will be discussed here, and this is certainly not an exhaustive list of the attacks on Obama that could be construed as subtle racial attacks. These are poignant examples that can serve to make the larger case about what meaning and significance can be gleaned from the attacks on Obama.

UNITED STATES CITIZENSHIP

Obama's citizenship was not only questioned early on in the campaign, but questions about his citizenship became the centerpiece of a full-fledged movement that exists to this day. People who questioned whether or not Obama is a U.S. citizen are referred to as "Birthers," and some of these people are a part of the "Birther Movement." Given that Obama was born in Hawaii and that he produced not only a birth certificate that was placed on the internet, as well as the fact that he also produced a newspaper birth announcement should have reassured the most skeptical "Birther" that Obama is a U.S. citizen. However, did not; thus, it is hard to believe that other factors did not contribute to this sustained movement that included even elected officials who openly questioned whether or not Obama was a U.S. citizen. Put in the context of Obama defeating a candidate, Senator John McCain, who was born in Panama, and the fact that this was rarely covered by the mainstream media or scrutinized publicly in the same way suggests a strong racial element present in this issue. Is it possible that it is simply easier to think that a Black man is not a citizen of the country? Given the fact that Hawaii is the most diverse state regarding population and that it is often associated with "exotic others" (ethnic Hawaiians), it also seems to be clear that this also plays a prominent role in this ongoing debate.

PATRIOTISM

This questioning of Obama's citizenship is closely linked to the attacks on his patriotism. Some of the more prominent attacks on his patriotism have been directed at his unwillingness to wear a flag lapel pin, his attendance at a "terrorist training" madrassa as part of his primary education in Indonesia, and his association with Bill Ayers, who was a former member of the Weather Underground Organization. These attacks start with the false narrative of Obama not being a U.S. citizen, and this then makes it much easier to believe that Obama is not interested in wearing an American flag lapel pin, that he was willing to attend a "terrorist school" (madrassa), and that he was willing to associate with "White terrorists." Obama spent part of his childhood in Indonesia, and he has not hidden this history. It was reported on FOX News that he attended a Muslim Madrassa and that this was a "terrorist training school" (Fox News, 2007). Steve Doocy on FOX News went so far as to say that Obama being raised as a "Muslim" was a "huge" story (Fox News, 2007). (The actual FOX News clip included in coverage by CNN as a web link: http://www.cnn.com/2007/POLITICS/01/22/obama.madrassa/ and Actual video clip of Steve Doocy's comments on Youtube: http://www.youtube.com/watch?v=nw6LBbeXTww) Of course, it was later reported that "madrassa" actually means "educational institution" and that the "Muslim terrorist madrassa" Obama attended really was not a "terrorist training camp," but a public school (Tapper & Venkataraman, 2007). Putting aside the likelihood that a major candidate running for president of the U.S. would probably not decide to run for office if he or she had attended a "terrorist training camp," the fact that FOX News and other networks actually picked up this story and covered it was remarkable. The mistake that FOX News made could have been corrected in a matter of seconds. Whether through a Google search of the word "madrassa" or asking any of the one billion Muslims in the world what this word meant, clearly these steps were not taken before it was reported that a major candidate running for president had attended a "terrorist training school" in Indonesia. It seemed to suggest that there was no limit to what some media outlets would and could report regarding Obama, and the typical process of verification of newsworthy items that mainstream media use seemed to been thrown out for this election cycle.

Two other notable incidents fit into this package of Obama as a "terrorist." One incident occurred early in Obama's Democratic Party nomination campaign when a picture of him was released in "African garb." During his trip to Kenya, Obama partook in the American political custom of wearing local clothes, and this picture reflects Obama's attempt to follow this practice (Sweet, 2008). One of these pictures was mysteriously released, and it was quickly seized upon by his detractors to illustrate his "otherness" (Juliano, 2008). On numerous occasions presidents and prominent politicians have dressed in the appropriate clothing for the place they are visiting, yet rarely has this common practice raised as much concern about a politician's identity and his/her patriotism. This was then not just a picture of Senator Obama at that time, but a picture of something that could be understood as foreign, dangerous, and not normal. It was a way to make Obama look like the Al Qaeda terrorists that the U.S. military was searching for and less like a credible candidate for the U.S. presidency.

An even more striking example of bizarre media attempts to turn Obama into a "terrorist" could be found in FOX News' report of a "terrorist jab" (MediaMatters for America, 2008). When Barack Obama took the stage after his wife Michelle had spoken, they exchanged a "fist bump" (MediaMatters for America, 2008). FOX News then proceeded to present this as a possible "terrorist fist bump" and suggested that this was a very provocative and unusual gesture (MediaMatters for America, 2008). Of course, if anyone from FOX News had asked anyone under the age of 25 (or asked any Black person, or any person who plays sports on a regular basis, or a person who watches comedy shows on television, etc.) it would have quickly concluded how ludicrous it was to present this routine and ordinary greeting as a "terrorist fist bump." FOX News did quickly retreat from this initial reporting, and most other networks did not follow FOX off this cliff.

Another attempt to tar Obama with the wide swath of the terrorist and terrorism brush was done with his association with Bill Ayers. Bill Ayers had hosted a fundraiser for Obama when he first ran for the Illinois State

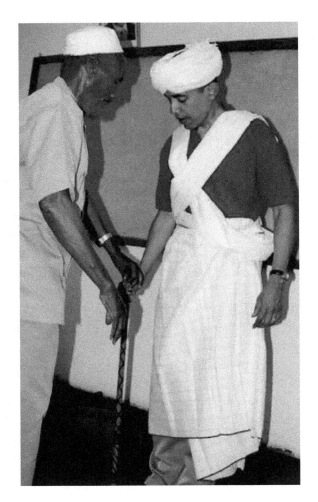

Fig. 4.6.

Senate office, and Ayers interacted with Obama throughout his political career in Illinois (Fusco & Pallasch, 2008). Part of this interaction was based on the fact that the Ayers were neighbors of the Obamas in the Hyde Park neighborhood of Chicago and that Ayers and Obama's work on education reform increased the probability that they would interact with each other (Smith, 2008). Bill Ayers was active in the Weather Underground Organization in his youth, and the most sensational incidents and actions that the Weather Underground was allegedly associated with were trotted out for display whenever Ayers and Obama were covered by the media. (Ayers also represents another significant trope for American culture, and one could also explore the radical/Communist/foreigner/traitor/Jew angle as well.) This peculiar fascination the McCain campaign and the media had with Ayers was remarkable if for no other reason than that it was the new standard they were using for character assassination by association. If the Ayers relationship with Obama was used as a way to measure and judge all politicians, then it is safe to say that most elected officials would suffer, and very few could pass this type of "purity test." For example, Keith Olbermann on MSNBC pointed out that a more compelling case could be made for Senator McCain meeting with "terrorists," yet this story was never presented and covered in the same way as the many stories about Obama's association with and ties to terrorists and terrorism. The ease with which a Black man can be put into a narrative of a subversive criminal and enemy of the state was not extraordinary when placed within a historical and political context in which so many African American leaders and celebrities are treated in a similar fashion.

The final example of a challenge to Obama's patriotism that had subtle racial overtones had to do with his apparent unwillingness to wear a flag lapel pin. Obama was asked why he did not wear a flag lapel pin in his public appearances. He answered this question by stating that he could more effectively express his patriotism by "speaking out on issues that are of importance to our national security" (FAIR [Fairness and Accuracy In Reporting], 2007). (FAIR (Fairness and Accuracy In Reporting): "Obama's 'Missing' Flag Pin Trivia Again Distracts Media From Issues Voters Care About," October 10, 2007.)

This did not stop many dominant media sources from analyzing Obama's many public appearances without the pin and selectively pointing out all of the occasions in which other candidates were wearing American flag lapel pins in public settings. There was even scrutiny of one occasion when Obama did not place his hand over his heart when the national anthem was being played. All of this seems to add to public construction of Obama as not a true patriot. What was extraordinary about this attack is that Obama was not the only candidate missing a U.S. flag lapel pin on a regular basis, but somehow these other candidates never received the same level of scrutiny (Wright & Miller, 2007).

CHRISTIAN FAITH AND HIS CHOICE OF CHURCH

A constant drumbeat of attacks focused on Obama's religious faith and practice. This was most noticeable in the attacks on his church, Trinity United Church of Christ, and its pastor, Reverend Jeremiah Wright (Ross & El-Buri, 2008). Once again the public was exposed to an excruciating examination of Obama's religious life, one that had never been conducted on any major political party candidate running for president. This included taking very short sound bites from Reverend Wright's sermons from as far back as twenty years past, as well as even questioning the church's "unabashedly" pro-Black mission statement (MediaMatters for America, 2007) (FAIR (Fairness and Accuracy In Reporting): "Obama's 'Missing' Flag Pin Trivia Again Distracts Media From Issues Voters Care About," October 10, 2007.) In particular, the media frenzy was most intense over the clip of Reverend Wright proclaiming "God damn America." Context meant nothing, and this and other notable sound bites were part of a 24-hour attack news cycle on perpetual loop (Martin, 2008). This news cycle ad-nauseam loop established a rock-solid narrative of a radical Black pastor who hates America, and that this was Obama's pastor (Seelye, 2008). Nobody analyzed Reverend Wright's extraordinary personal history, which included not only serving in the Marine Corps but also being a part of the medical team that treated President Lyndon Johnson, nor was there an analysis of how Reverend Wright and Trinity United Church of Christ fit into the larger mainstream matrix of Black pastors and churches that have similar theological and political leanings (Martin, 2008). What was most extraordinary about the intensity of this attack on Obama's pastor and church was how exceptional it was in terms of coverage of other candidates' religion. No other candidate received the same scrutiny, and, in fact, in the case of Senator McCain or Senator Clinton someone would be hard pressed to name their churches and/or pastors. Historically even presidents with note-worthy churches and pastors never received the same level of scrutiny. For example, President Jimmy Carter attended a White-only church in Georgia (Bailey, 2007). The common practice of leaving a certain amount of privacy for a candidate's religious life was completely shattered with Obama.

BIRTH NAME

Of course, Obama's middle name, Hussein, received a great deal of scrutiny and ridicule (Thornburgh, 2008), not just because the U.S. had been fighting a war in Iraq and the former leader of that country was named Saddam Hussein, but even on an a more rudimentary level because the name was foreign and Arab/Muslim. It was not long before this middle name became an insult and was used by conservatives to convey their intense hatred and distrust of Obama (MediaMatters for America, 2006) (MediaMatters for America, "Tucker Carlson on Obama's Church: "[I]t's Hard to Call that Christianity," February 9, 2007. Retrieved from http://mediamatters. org/research/200702090009 and MediaMatters for America, "Fox News' E.D. Hill Teased Discussion of Obama Dap: "A Fist Bump? A pPound? A Terrorist Fist Jab?" June 6, 2008. Retrieved from http://mediamatters.org/ mmtv/200806060007) The focus on Obama's name was a marked departure from traditional political discourse. Typically, when candidates' names are used for attack, it is in terms of humor, not as a part of an assault on their citizenship and patriotism. Given the fact that a birth name is not something a candidate can control (without legally changing his/her name), then it follows that attacks that are solely based on a candidate's name are not only personal assaults, but these types of attacks are also disconnected from actual policy positions and political views that candidates should be responsible for producing and presenting as part of their campaigns.

These attacks on where he was born, what schools he attended, and the name he was given at birth were much more about a fundamental attack on Obama's identity than on his political party or positions on issues or political career accomplishments and failures. From this vantage point I would argue that these areas served as a proxy for the more fundamental racial identity that could not necessarily be attacked openly. Whereas overt and crude racial attacks were launched against Obama, just as many people who were not as comfortable with making these attacks relied on proxy or shorthand attacks on his name, birthplace, primary education, or even his church and his pastor. In deciding between the traditional attacks that are leveled at the Democratic Party and Democratic Party candidates, such as "tax-and-spend liberals," being weak on the war on terrorism, and mismanagement of the economy, it is striking to see how often individuals and organizations deviated from these attacks and went into the realm of overt and subtle racism. Based on the amount and the intensity of these racial attacks, it is hard to believe that some type of calculation was not made about the nature of the attacks and the specific prospects of success based on the choice of attacks. An examination of these overt and subtle areas of attack clearly illustrates that they were not just a typical or normal exchange that transpired and that ugly racial dynamics were in play. Given the extent that typical discourse was tossed out the window and a brutal racial discourse was interjected, one could argue that this was a very sad and predictable outcome.

YOUTH ATTACKS

Notable racist attacks were launched at the president by youth and students. These attacks serve as another barometer for race relations in this country. In part, the concept of racial progress and a post-racial narrative is built upon the premise of a noticeable change in attitude toward race and racism among youth and young adults. However, the presence of sizeable and frequent racial attacks by youth directed at President Obama would severely undermine this narrative. The adolescent years are a critical time for the development of racial attitudes and beliefs. For a child or a teenager to express either overt or subtle racial biases or beliefs would suggest that this was part of learned behavior, especially if the expression of racism is in a public setting, and it is intentional. These racist views must have come from something in the young person's environment—or perhaps was something biological, some view or belief the person was born with. Placed within this context, the incidents that took place at the University of Arizona and the University of Mississippi are worth examining.

The incident at the University of Mississippi was described as spontaneous reaction to the news that Obama had won the 2012 election. A small group of students grew to a crowd of hundreds of students. The students chanted political slogans, but they used racial epithets to express their views. The use of derogatory racial language does not suggest a traditional shift in presidential power or the simple ushering in of a new president. Part of this racial reaction by the students at Ole Miss can be traced back to the racialized election tactics and strategies that were utilized against Obama, as well as the school's own history. In fact, this racist incident took place just after the 50th anniversary of the attempt by James Meredith to integrate Ole Miss with its first Black student. President Kennedy ultimately had to utilize U.S. Marshals to quell the massive race riots on campus and safely complete the integration process for James Meredith. Many other key historical racial landmarks can be noted for Ole Miss, and it is important to highlight that some of these landmarks are a part of more recent history: In 1997 the school put an official end to waving Confederate flags at sporting events, and in 2003 the Colonel Reb mascot, based on a White male plantation owner, was replaced. Given the history of Ole Miss, it is not surprising that this campus would be one of the sites of overtly racist protests of the election of Obama in 2012. Ole Miss was not the only school that was reported to have an overtly racist reaction on election night. Another racist incident occurred at Hampden-Sydney College in Virginia when a group of students congregated around the Minority Student Union house and proceed to scream out racial insults. This group of about 40 students also set off fireworks and broke bottles.

Hampden-Sydney College is a small, all-male school with just over 1,000 students, but it is not immune from the same type of racial discourse that has plagued much larger schools, such as the University of Mississippi. Given that this is what has been reported by mainstream press sources about the reaction of students at two schools to the election of the first African American president for a second term, what does this response from the students reveal about their own racial views and actions? How significant of a shift of racial attitudes and behaviors has occurred in the last fifty years, and how exceptional was this reaction to other college campuses and for students and young adults in general? What are the racial attitudes and behaviors young White males and females are being exposed to, and what does this tell us about what racial outlooks might be developed as youth moves into adulthood?

Fig. 4.7. Sign Burning at Ole Miss Riot

Another incident occurred outside of Desert Vista High School in Phoenix in 2013 when Obama spoke at this high school. It was noted in the press that some of the protesters directed racial slurs and racially tinged attacks at Obama. Some of the examples of these racist attacks included the singing of "Bye Bye Black Sheep" to make a derogatory reference to Obama's racial identity and signs and comments, such as "Impeach the Half-White Muslim!" and "He's 47% percent Negro" (Merrill, Nanez, & Bennett, 2013, p. 1). A University of Arizona student who was carrying the sign "Impeach the Half-White Muslim!" not only defended the message conveyed by her sign, but she also went so far as to suggest to the media that "Obama supporters use(d) the 'race card' against her because they disagreed with her political message" (Merrill, Nanez, & Bennett, p. 1). What is particularly troubling about this response is that the very idea of identifying and challenging racism is called into question. It is not surprising that the full quotation presented by Merrill, Nanez, and Bennett suggests that this student's response brings her rationale for the use of this sign to its logical and ironic racist endpoint:

> "Obama is ruining American values. He is ruining the Constitution. He needs to go back to where he came from because, obviously, he is a liar," she said. "I am not racist. I am part Indian. Obama's half Black, half White" (p. 1).

On the one hand, this student can defend the message "Impeach the Half-White Muslim!" on first the grounds that to contest or challenge this message would be racist itself, while on the other hand she grounds the legitimacy and fairness of her use of this language because of her own partial-racial-minority identity. What is fascinating about this logic is that if this same student was denied a job, the right to vote, a home to live in, or any other American right to liberty or justice, this student would most likely contest this discrimination on racial grounds. She would also most likely not be concerned with whether the person or people discriminating against her were White or non-White, and she would certainly accept this treatment as being acceptable based on any similarly held racial-identity grounds. It is also worth noting that the comments about Obama ruining American values and the Constitution, as well as the comment about Obama needing to go back to where he came from, are also a very overt racist diatribe. Without the context of an African American president that has been racially attacked for being a secret Muslim and Kenyan-born, this form of critique would have no meaning or significance. Setting aside this racist rant and the logical fallacies of the previous argument, it is important to appreciate the appeal and currency these ideas have now for large segments of White and non-White youth and young adults. That youth and young adults lack the analytical tools to identify and understand how race and racism operate in society is a worrisome trend. Youth and young adults can literally be drawn into what might be presented as a "neutral" political setting (a protest of a president) and the event can easily become marred by racist discourse (the use of racism to attack the president). These racist attacks launched by youth against Obama provide insights into how race and racism can be passed to a new generation. In a similar fashion as the previously discussed racist images and messages, the youth examples draw from the well of race and racism, and they produce images and messages that would appear to be a part of a bygone era. The fact that these forms of racism still resonate with a segment of youth today does not bode well for those who use a post-racial doctrine to explain the current racial climate and relations. To the extent that a new generation of youth will be influenced by and gain meaning from overt and subtle forms of racism, this type of racial discourse will likely continue to be a part of the U.S. societal fabric.

RACIAL ATTACKS FROM TEA PARTY ACTIVISTS

The start of the Tea Party movement in 2009 and the openly racist material, actions, and messages presented at their functions were examples of this type of overt and subtle assault (Hennessey & Memoli, 2010). One of the most notorious incidents that took place at a Tea Party rally in Washington, DC was when members of the congressional Black caucus accused participants of this rally of using racial epithets and spitting on them (Kane, Paul & Stein).

Fig. 4.8.

This picture (Fig. 4.8) provides a glimpse into the setting and the dynamics of this explosive Tea Party rally. It was during this time when congressional Black caucus members walked through the rally on the way to the Capitol that they claim some members were spat upon and that racial insults were screamed at them.

Even though this incident was exceptional in the severity and level of scrutiny it received, key elements of this Tea Party rally were noticeable in most all of the events that were coordinated directly by Tea Party organizations and their affiliate groups. The signs, images, and messaging at these events provided some of the foundational elements. *The Huffington Post* provided a pictorial montage from Tea Party function signs that were

Fig. 4.9a.

Fig. 4.9b.

Fig. 4.10.

Fig. 4.11.

held by the participants in these actions. Many of these signs used overt and subtle messages and images.

The way that specific political grievances and differences of opinion on policies became ensnarled in this corrosive racial discourse is fascinating. One could simply ask, *what were these people gathering for and what did they expect to accomplish?* Based on many of the signs, one could conclude that these were "racist rallies" directed at President Obama, as opposed to rallies organized to oppose or support specific public policies. The fact that one rally was organized for proposed healthcare reform legislation is very difficult to ascertain from the messages, symbols, and images used on the signs many of the participants waved. This raises the question of why the images and messages were used within this political context and if this was an effective and practical way to address the Tea Party's objectives. In other words, if their goal was to stop or alter healthcare reform, is showing Obama slashing Uncle Sam's throat (Fig. 4.9a-b), or using Gary Coleman's line from *Diff'rent Strokes*, "What ya talking about, Willis?" (Fig. 4.10), or referring to Obama's policies as White Slavery (Fig. 4.11) the most effective and useful political tactic? Specifically, if one starts with the sign of Obama cutting Uncle Sam's throat, then it is possible to see the very stark racial images used and messaged conveyed. Obama is portrayed as the dangerous, dark, scary Black man, and he is literally killing the beloved, sacred patriarch, Uncle

Sam. The next sign utilizes a message from a popular television show from the late 1970s and early 1980s. Gary Coleman's character, Arnold, had the memorable line for his old bother Willis, played by Todd Bridges, "What ya talking about, Willis?" when he wanted to express dismay, surprise, and/or distrust. The use of this line for a Tea Party political rally suggests that not only did the comedy show with African American teenagers as the primary characters still have some type of tributary value, but that specific line resonated as a way to ridicule and belittle the current occupant of the White House. The last sign presented the "White Slavery" message, and it is very easy to understand the overt racial overtones of this message. With a Black president, it was assumed that there was a shared audience for the legitimate fear of White slavery. Even used as an attempt at humor, the sign is equally troubling as an attempt at a serious political message. The underlying assumption would be that some part of the audience would relate to the use of White slavery to highlight the fact that a president who is racially connected to a group of people who came to America as slaves. One could surmise that the racial discourse superseded any simple political agenda, and the opportunity to level an overt or subtle racist message at President Obama was paramount. This conclusion could be reached by analyzing the tangible political goals that were accomplished by the Tea Party. The legislation ultimately passed and significant changes were made in the way health care is delivered to millions of Americans. If the work of the Tea Party in this respect was not effective, then it is fair to ask why didn't they organize events in opposition to health care reform that carried no overt or covert racist messages directed at President Obama? More to the point, would it not have been more effective to have signs and messaging at these rallies that pointed out specific weaknesses and faults with the proposed legislation? Since this was not done, then it is also fair to ask why the signs and messaging for their events were deeply entrenched in a racist discourse and what this means for how race and racism operate in our society.

The Institute for Research and Education on Human Rights issued a report called "Tea Party Nationalism," and the report used "news articles, visits to white nationalist Web sites and observance of tea party functions to claim that tea party events have become a forum for extremists 'hoping to push these (white) protesters toward a more self-conscious and ideological white supremacy'" (Institute for Research & Education on Human Rights, 2010). The previous examples and analysis of three signs utilized by participants at a Tea Party rally support this conclusion. The focal point becomes a shared racial bonding that is seamlessly drawn together through opposition to President Obama with emphasis on his racial identity, the use of overt and covert signs, symbols, and messaging, and an audience that shares an appetite for this type of racial discourse and derives meaning and sustenance from it.

RACIAL ATTACK FROM ELECTED OFFICIALS

These examples also connect with the Subtle and Overt racist messages that have been delivered by current and past elected officials. An example could be Congressman Joe Wilson's interruption of Obama during a speech to a joint session of Congress and his use of "You lie!" to interrupt and attack the president (Hooper, 2009). Michael Scherer (2009) described this event in the following manner: "So when Representative Joe Wilson, a little-known Republican and Army Reserve veteran from South Carolina shouted them at the nation's Commander in Chief on the night of Sept. 9, heads snapped. The House chamber took a collective gasp" (p. 2). It was not just a sitting member of Congress shouting at the president of the United States during one of our most sacrosanct political functions, but it was in the context of the first African American president during the first year of his Presidency receiving this level of hostility. It was a remarkable departure from typical political decorum. The fact that this interruption to the president's speech came from an extremely conservative White male congressman from the Second District of South Carolina added the element of the unsavory racial legacy.

This racial element was succinctly encapsulated at the beginning of Maureen Dowd's 2009 column.

> Surrounded by middle-aged white guys—a sepia snapshot of the days when such pols ran Washington like their own men's club—Joe Wilson yelled "You lie!" at a president who didn't. But, fair or not, what I heard was an unspoken word in the air: You lie, boy! (p. 1)

To support the racial epithet that she heard but was not actually uttered, Dowd provides a discussion of Wilson's record. This record lends credence to the racialized climate in which Wilson delivered these comments and the message he attempted to convey.

Dowd's (2009) point about how "boy" might as well have been tagged on to end of his comments can be understood when these parts of Wilson's history are included in an analysis of this incident: "The congressman, we learned, belonged to the Sons of Confederate Veterans, led a 2000 campaign to keep the Confederate flag waving above South Carolina's state Capitol, and denounced as a 'smear' the true claim of a black woman that she was the daughter of Strom Thurmond, the '48 segregationist candidate for president" (p. 1). These historically significant racial components of Wilson's background suggest that this was not just a case of a congressman breaking with the decorum and tradition of congressional behavior in receiving a presidential address. This racialized context then needs to be included in any thoughtful analysis of this incident, and it also allows for an analysis of other incidents to be examined in a similar fashion. The racialized discourse that plagued Obama during the Democratic party nomination battle in 2007 and 2008 continued while he was in office as president. Elected political leaders also played a critical role in the way that this discourse was constructed and often provided some of the most significant contributions to this discourse.

Another example that could be included in this grouping of racial assaults can be seen in the picture of the White House with a watermelon patch that was distributed by a Republican mayor (Fig. 4.12).

Even with this overt form of racism, similar attempts were made to downplay and disown any racial elements. The explanation Mayor Grose offered in his press interview is described in the following manner:

Fig. 4.12.

"He said he was unaware of the racial stereotype that black people like watermelons" (CBS News, 2009). (CBS News, "Mayor Hits Rough Patch Over Watermelon Pic," February 25, 2009.Retrieved from http://www.cbsnews.com/stories/2009/02/25/national/main4827964.shtml).   This appeared to be sufficient, and this was barely a one-day media story. When connected to Congressman Wilson's outburst, one can begin to track Overt and Subtle forms of racist attack on the president. Regardless of the knowledge and/or intent of these racial attacks, a very clear and consistent pattern of racial assaults emerges.

More overt racially tinged comments were directed at President Obama, and Congresswoman Lynn Jenkins' comment about a Great White Hope provides an easy example of how this level of racism manifested. She offered the following insight at a meeting of followers in Hiawatha, Kansas: "Republicans are struggling right now to find the great white hope. I suggest to any of you who are concerned about that who are Republican, there are some great young Republican minds in Washington" (Kornreich, 2009). Jenkins was a freshman Republican representing the Topeka, Kansas area when she made these inflammatory comments on August 19, 2009. In case it was not clear what her "White Hope" reference was based on, the following background was provided by Tim Carpenter (2009): "The phrase 'great white hope' is frequently tied to racist attitudes permeating the United States when heavyweight boxing champion Jack Johnson fought in the early 1900s" (p. 1). Carpenter (2009) goes on to add, "Reaction to the first black man to reign as champion was intense enough to build support for a campaign to find a white fighter capable of reclaiming the title from Johnson" (p. 1). The fact that to explain her comments she had to offer historical lessons about race and racism in this country speaks volumes as to exactly how this process continues to be played out in the media. On one level, at face value, this comment could be interpreted as amusing and harmless, especially without an understanding or appreciation of the historical legacy surrounding the comment. On another level, to be able to give some meaning and value to this comment, one needs to work through a rich racial history that accompanies this term. References made to finding a "Great White Hope" to fight Jack Johnson in the 1900s are more likely to be familiar for an older population and one that either lived through that time period or was raised by and exposed to people who lived through that period. For a Republican candidate or elected official who relied on primarily older, White males as his/her basis of political support, comments about a "Great White Hope" are more likely to resonate. It should not be surprising that Jenkins selected this term to convey to her base constituency the perceived battle with President Obama, and she went on to mention White male Republicans who could run against Obama. Placing the presidential election in a racialized context was not an accident, and it was based on perceived political advantage.

The next example of racist comments and terms used again President Obama provides a logical extension of the "Great White Hope" comments into an operational method for the "Great White Hope" Republican candidate to challenge President Obama on overt racialized level. Former Speaker of the House and Republican presidential candidate Newt Gingrich used the term "Food Stamp President" in the 2012 presidential election, providing another example of how this destructive racial discourse for president was constructed and maintained. On one level, Bjerga and Oldham's (2012) discussion of Gingrich's use of the term would seem to be standard political fodder: "Gingrich, a former congressman from Georgia and Speaker of the House, said yesterday on NBC's 'Today' show, that he began calling Obama the food-stamp president in the 2010 election cycle" and "He said the president's policies 'have put more Americans on food stamps than any president in history'" (p. 1). The added element of historical context and racial discourse puts the use of this term in a very different light and moves it out of the realm of a simple attack message for political consumption.

As suggested by Bjerga and Oldham (2012), the specific use of this term can be seen as not just patently false, but also intentionally racially divisive: "From 1970 until about a decade ago, average annual [food stamp] enrollment rose or fell roughly with economic conditions" (p. 2). Bjerga and Oldham (2012) then point out that the food stamp rate has actually "declined only once since then, partly because policies adopted under President George W. Bush encouraged more eligible people to apply for aid, said David Armor, a professor emeritus of public policy at George Mason University in Fairfax, Virginia" (p. 2). If it is well understood that food stamp subscriptions rise with poor economic conditions and that the catastrophic economic conditions we went through in 2008–2009 correlate with the increase in food stamp recipients, then the president in office during this time would bear no responsibility for this spike in recipients eligible for food stamps. If you add this to the fact that during the Bush administration that the eligibility standards for food stamps were loosened, then it becomes very clear how profoundly inaccurate the use of this label was for President Obama. In the same article by Bjerga and Oldham, a quote from David Greenberg provides the likely explanation for why this term was used by Gingrich: "I don't think he is consciously whipping up bigotry, but he is no fool, and this is going to be seen through a racial prism" (p. 2). The point is that Gingrich, a former congressman from Georgia, was cognizant of the racial universe into which he unleashed this political attack. The association of the first African American president with food stamps is a very potent racial weapon to utilize. It presents the president as pushing benefits for poor, underserved African Americans at a time when the economy of the country was still substantially weakened. Those looking for work and those receiving meager benefits could identify with this term and coalescence around the racial enemy of African Americans unfairly using these government benefits.

This is also why Gingrich's comments were compared to President Reagan's use of "welfare queen" to describe those receiving welfare benefits. The shift then is the target of racial attack (from receipts of the service to the president) and the implications of this type of attack (attack on a program based on racialized image as opposed to an attack on presidential decorum and tradition). What is more difficult to assess is the qualitative racial damage that this type of shift has on African Americans and racial minorities in general. With the president occupying the space of the racial other, it was not necessary for Gingrich to develop a term to describe a generic food-stamp recipient to attack the program or to make the political point about the increase in the use of the program. He could instead directly attack the president and make him an embodiment of the program, not just a member of a political party that has support-ed this program. Gingrich made a political choice to not just attack the food-stamp program and/or the president, but to do it in a way that was couched in a racialized discourse. This use of language and images also extended to personal contact with the president, and this level of personal and public interaction can be seen as the logical extension of this racial-ized discourse.

The most notable example of a public exchange between an elected official and President Obama that can be understood as having racial con-nation occurred when Arizona Governor Jan Brewer decided to point her finger in the president's face as they seem to be engaged in a very heated exchange (Fig. 4.13). Questions about the uniqueness of the moment of a public official wagging her finger in the president's face and why the first African American president provided this opening have to be asked.

This picture of Governor Jan Brewer pointing her finger in the face of President Barack Obama after he arrived in Mesa on Wednesday, Jan. 25, 2012, is an excellent example of how the boundaries of customary and acceptable decorum made a remarkable shift with our first African American president. It is also worth noting that with the previous president,

Fig. 4.13.

George W. Bush, the Secret Service removed people from events based on bumper stickers and shirts that were deemed unacceptable. It would be difficult to imagine what would have occurred if a public official waved a finger in the face of President Bush or any other previous occupant of the White House. This personal level of interaction with President Obama combining racist language and images begins to paint a picture of how much presidential decorum and traditions have been stretched. These examples also begin to portray the racialized discourse that seeps into these interactions, images, and language used with President Obama. Another layer of this analysis can be added when the First Lady and the president's family are also included.

RACIAL ASSAULTS DIRECTED AT FIRST LADY MICHELLE OBAMA

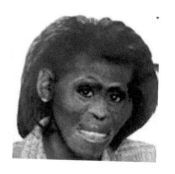

Fig. 4.14. Photoshopped Image of Michelle Obama, 2009.

It is not surprising to find that the racist attacks directed at President Obama encompassed his family, too. Although little research has been done on attacks directed at First Ladies, it safe to conclude that First Lady Michelle Obama also encountered distinctly different types of attacks from any other First Lady. Just as the attacks directed at her husband plowed new ground, the same can be said about the overt and subtle racist attacks Michelle Obama has experienced. Questions about to what extent these attacks fit within comfortable boundaries for decorum and tradition for First Ladies cannot be addressed in a systematic and conclusive fashion. What is most intriguing is the fact that a specific strain of racist attacks has been directed at both of the Obamas with striking similarities in the images and the language used within this racial discourse of attacks. The attacks directed at Michelle Obama started at an early point in the presidential election campaign for her husband, and they continued through both terms in office.

The first noteworthy racist image is based on monkey imagery (Fig. 4.14), and this image began to set the tone for the racist tropes used against Michelle Obama, just as it had been used against Barack Obama.

Unfortunately, this racist imagery has not been restricted to the president. In November 2009, a photoshopped racist image of First Lady Michelle Obama made international news. There were, and are, plenty of racist images on the Internet of Mr. and Mrs. Obama. What made this particular image such a big story was that it ranked first on Internet giant Google's image search page. (The Coon Caricature: Blacks as Monkeys, Photoshopped Image of Michelle Obama, 2009.)

The key point about this image is its popularity and wide level of exposure. If this was just an innocent joke or typical funny political antics, then why was there such a substantial appetite for this image as suggested by the Google search engine records? Since this image so directly harkens back to a time in our country when these images were prominent and acceptable, then what does it say about our current racial climate that such an extensive audience exists for these types of racial caricatures to be used to present the First Lady and the president? Part of the simple answers to these questions has to start with the novelty of these actions and images for a president. No previous occupant of the White House had his racial identity challenged and belittled, as well as his wife and relatives. One could also conclude that this type of attack was not done because of presidential decorum and tradition as previously covered, as well as the minimal political advantage that might be gained by these attacks. Put another way, would these racist attacks occur spontaneously or in a random fashion if no perceived political advantage could be attached to them? Given that no noticeable political harm was caused by the perpetrators or the political party and movement they are associated with, then what is the likelihood that these attacks would cease or decrease in volume and/ or intensity?

Another example of the way Michelle Obama was presented was as a Black radical, and one version of this racial trope could be seen in the visual presentation of her as "Angela Davis" (Fig. 4.15). The most

Fig. 4.15. *The New Yorker* July 21st, 2008 Cover

remarkable representation was displayed on the cover of *The New Yorker* on July 21, 2008.

Since the work of Barry Blitt appeared on the cover of a magazine that is associated with liberal and intellectual thought, it was defended in the following manner, as described by Rachel Sklar (2008): "The illustration, by Barry Blitt, is called 'The Politics of Fear' and, according to the *NYer* press release, 'satirizes the use of scare tactics and misinformation in the presidential election to derail Barack Obama's campaign.' Uh-huh. What's that they say about repeating a rumor?" (p. 1). Even within the frame of a satirical presentation of the Obamas based on right-wing conservative views of them, questions could be asked about the genesis of these views of the Obamas, why this particular image was selected and presented this way by *The New Yorker*, and how effective is it as a political tactic to re-package and re-distribute these images as satire.

IMAGE CREDITS

- Fig. 4.1: Copyright © 2008 by USA Today.
- Fig. 4.2: Copyright © 2008 by The Washington Post.
- Fig. 4.3: Copyright © 2008 by Hearst Seattle Media, LLC.
- Fig. 4.4: Source: http://www.huffingtonpost.com/chip-berlet/bigoted-obama-waffles-pac_b_126404.html
- Fig. 4.5: Copyright © 2008 by ThinkProgress.
- Fig. 4.6: Source: http://www.politico.com/story/2008/02/obama-slams-smear-photo-008667.
- Fig. 4.7: Source: http://www.salon.com/2012/11/07/ole_miss_students_start_racist_protest_after_election_result/
- Fig. 4.8: Source: https://i.ytimg.com/vi/-SCs6pSE8_I/hqdefault.jpg.
- Fig. 4.9a: Source: http://www.huffingtonpost.com/2013/10/24/tea-party-racist_n_4158262.html.
- Fig. 4.9b: Source: http://wunschelreport.blogspot.com/2010/08/wrong-kind-of-change.html
- Fig. 4.10: Source: http://www.huffingtonpost.com/2013/10/24/tea-party-racist_n_4158262.html.
- Fig. 4.11: Source: http://www.huffingtonpost.com/2013/10/24/tea-party-racist_n_4158262.html.
- Fig. 4.12: Source: http://www.womanistmusings.com/watermelons-at-whitehouse-and/
- Fig. 4.13: Source: http://www.cbsnews.com/news/jan-brewer-gets-an-earful-from-obama-in-ariz/
- Fig. 4.14: Source: https://theawl.com/primate-in-chief-a-guide-to-racist-obama-monkey-photoshops-d31499c602e5#.c6abvx3s5.
- Fig. 4.15: from The New Yorker. Copyright © 2008 by Condé Nast Publications.

RACE, RACISM, AND THE EXECUTIVE BRANCH

After meeting with young black men from the Hyde Park Academy, Obama drew some knowing laughter when he noted, "A lot of them have had some issues." But the president stressed his kinship with them. "I had issues too when I was their age. I just had an environment that was a little more forgiving. So when I screwed up, the consequences weren't as high as when kids on the South Side screw up. So I had more of a safety net. But these guys are no different than me. "

Condon & O'Sullivan, 2013

INTRODUCTION

THEORETICAL AND METHODOLOGICAL RUPTURE

The previously cited scholarly work on negative campaigning can be reviewed in light of these examples of racist attacks on Obama. In particular,

Buell, Jr. and Sigelman's methodological and theoretical work can serve as potent examples of how traditional scholarship in the area of negative campaigning does provide the proper analytical and research tools for the Obama campaigns and presidency. To illustrate this point, it is worth returning to the previous discussion of the methodological and theoretical work done in the field of negative campaigning. It is now possible to review how applicable this work might be in general for how race and racism operate and are manifested in presidential elections, as well as how useful this work might be for specific examples of racist attacks leveled at Obama. The following questions need to be addressed: "Can these commonly utilized scholarly tools for evaluating negative campaigning properly account for and evaluate race and racism in presidential elections? If they cannot properly account for and explain the way that race and racism have operated for the Obama presidency, what needs to be developed and utilized to address this area?"

To be able to address this question, it is worthwhile to examine the previously discussed methodological and theoretical selections made by Buell, Jr. and Sigelman in their work on negative campaigning.

The way negative campaigning is defined is most significant, and this definition process determines the way in which this subject can be studied. The previous discussion of Buell, Jr. and Sigelman's work included an explanation of how and why they selected and utilized their definition of this term (Buell & Sigelman, 2008). Specifically, they made a distinction between negative campaigning that is based on valid and fair differences between candidates and the use of "wild, unsubstantiated charges" and how the former would serve as the basis of their scholarly work (Buell & Sigelman, 2008). The inherent subjective nature in the operational practice of this term was also noted. Very few campaigns would openly admit to the use of "wild, unsubstantiated charges." The ability to decipher and make definitive statements about negative campaigns would suggest an ability to access a level of objective truth and a way to utilize this truth for a methodologically sound practice. This part of their research does not resemble an exact science, and for each of the examples Buell and Sigelman refer to as "negative campaigns," they present a specific case to explain why they made the selection. They tie these examples into a larger social, political, and economic setting (Buell & Sigelman, 2008). This then matched their selection of a methodological approach that was based on "campaign statements extracted via a systematic coding procedure from every news item published in the *New York Times* about the presidential campaigns of 1960 to 2008" (Buell & Sigelman, 2008). They developed then not just a definition for negative campaigning that allowed for them to decide on what material was worthy of collection and a process for collecting this material, but they also developed an analytical model to assess the rationale for why and when this negative campaigning was utilized. The use of the Skaperdas-Grofman model created the space for Buell and Sigelman's negative campaign observations to be neatly tracked, classified, and evaluated.

When racial attacks and dynamics are introduced, the explanatory power of the work done by Buell and Sigelman is greatly diminished. The previous discussion of racist attacks provides an invaluable way to highlight the weaknesses in Buell and Sigelman's approach. In particular, the Subtle and Overt racial categories present formidable obstacles. The Overt racial attacks (Obama's image placed on waffle boxes with a similar expression as an Aunt Jemima character, Obama's image on fake money with the caption "Obama Bucks" and a picture of watermelon and a bucket of fried chicken in the background, an Obama image as an Arab with a turban on a three-dollar bill, Obama's image on a "Curious George" shirt with the slogan "Obama '08," and a button suggesting that the White House will need a name change if Obama were elected) would not even be detected and evaluated within a framework that relied on the central tenets of Buell and Sigelman's work. The previous discussion about how to define negative campaigning can be seen in a different light now. From the vantage point of racist campaign material or incidents these forms of racism might be excluded from negative campaign research based on the established definitional boundaries. If it is difficult enough to be able to determine if a negative campaign is "mudslinging" or a valid critique of policy, then making a determination about the racist nature of an attack would amplify this difficulty to a potentially unmanageable level. The question of claiming that a campaign used a racist advertisement or statement would be even more difficult to, first, identify, and, second, determine the value and rationale for this attack. When applied to the 2008 election, the Overt racial attacks could pass the first hurdle of being labeled racist and even be included as part of the overall campaign strategy and tactics utilized by Obama's opponents, but another critical part of Buell and Sigelman's work would need to be addressed by these racial attacks. This then leads to a discussion of the second example of a challenge for defining negative campaigning. This specific challenge relates to how Buell and Sigelman's work establish acceptable research boundaries for what can constitute as the source and the deliverer of negative campaign messages and what this practice would mean for racist campaign messages and incidents. Put simply, Buell and Sigelman claim that, "Although almost everyone accepts that negative campaigning means criticizing or attacking a rival candidate, slate, or party during a contest for elected office, no such consensus holds when the same researchers measure the prevalence of negativity in particular campaigns" (Buell and Sigelman, p. 3, 2008). This statement highlights the dilemma scholars who want to include racial attacks will face. These Overt attacks did not come from "traditional" channels (other candidate(s), official surrogates, or the oppositional party structure), nor were they directed at substantial policy or personality differences between the candidates. This might lead one to suggest that they should simply be disregarded and not utilized in formal negative campaign research. However, another way to understand and incorporate these attacks can serve as a supplement for what scholars, such as Buell and Sigelman, have contributed to this field.

Whereas the Overt Racism might be dismissed as crude, exceptional, and beneath normal campaign standards, and henceforth a case could be made for scholars to neglect this area, the same does not hold true for the Subtle Racism examples. The Subtle Racism examples cannot be dismissed in the same fashion, and the combination of both areas of racism demonstrates the potency and novelty of such racist negative campaigning. The Subtle racial attacks (Obama's Hawaiian birth certificate providing the basis to question his citizenship, challenging his patriotism because of the absence of a flag lapel pin and his past relationship to someone involved in the Weather Underground, attendance at a school in Indonesia that was labeled a "Muslim terrorist madrassa," attacks on his religious faith, his pastor, and his church membership in Trinity United Church of Christ, and his full birth name: Barack Hussein Obama) could meet the standard established by Buell and Sigelman while also providing some of the same definitional obstacles that the Overt forms met. On one level, some of these attacks could be classified as standard and acceptable components of campaigns in terms of the Subtle Racism being generated by traditional sources (e.g., oppositional candidates) and directed at commonly accepted targets (e.g., patriotism as way to challenge national security issues and positions), but on another level, all of the attacks did not fit neatly into the categories and analytical frames utilized for studying negative campaigning. An example of this can be seen in the attacks on Obama's patriotism; these attacks were considered "fair game." Attacking an opponent's patriotism has been a staple of national campaigns, and Obama was no exception to this type of attack. These attacks could also be considered ones that moved into a racial realm of significance given the context in which they were executed and understood. For example, in terms of the absent flag lapel pin, it was clear that Obama was singled out for this attack, and other candidates did not receive the same level of scrutiny for this issue (Wright & Miller, 2007). Thus, the fact that other candidates that were not wearing a flag lapel pin did not receive the same form of attacks and the same level of scrutiny draws attention to Obama's racial identity. This also holds true for the Subtle attacks in the other areas (church membership and pastor, terrorist school and friends, and birth country), and it was obvious that one standard was established for acceptable areas of attack for Obama and that none of the other candidates were attacked in these same areas, nor were they attacked in the same way. As previously mentioned, Buell and Sigelman suggest that, "Other things being equal, credible charges pack a bigger punch than patent falsehoods, but the difficulty of determining degrees of untruth in many, if not most, instances is insuperable. The same holds true of efforts to determine the fairness of attacks (assuming fairness can be distinguished from accuracy)." This type of logic should have led to the attacks on Obama's patriotism not being used for negative campaigns, or they should have been used equally against every candidate who was not wearing a flag lapel pin, who was born in the U.S., had terrorist friends, attended a terrorist school, etc. (Buell & Sigelman, 2008). In other words, if Buell and Sigelman's analytical approach were to apply to Obama, then there would have to be some way to reconcile and explain the rationale for the attacks launched at Obama and not at any of the other candidates that shared the same basic uncontroversial personal "truths" in terms of American identity, church, patriotism, school, friends, etc. (Buell & Sigelman, 2008). It appears that Obama was attacked regardless of what "truths" he might have shared with other candidates who avoided such scrutiny and attacks. In hindsight, this becomes an even more poignant issue since Obama won the Democratic primary and the general election yet was the only one subjected to this level of negative campaigning. A theory, such as the Skaperdas-Grofman model, premised on rational actors in the political arena with the single goal of election victory, could lead one to believe that racist attacks would not be utilized and would not be successful (in terms of an assessment of truth and fairness). Even if the Skaperdas-Grofman was presented in a framework that incorporated race and racism, and it was accepted that some racist negative campaigning (Overt and Subtle) would be useful and effective in national campaigns, then the fact that they were not successful in the 2008 elections would still have to be properly explained.

This highlights the overarching question about the way in which race and racism operate in society and the specific limitations for negative campaign research. This can be seen most clearly in the commentary that Buell and Sigelman offer about race and racism in the 2008 election. Buell and Sigelman (2008) start by saying, "Race ranked fairly high on both attack agendas, and it would have gotten even more play had the McCain campaign decided to make an issue of Obama's long relationship with his pastor, the Reverend Jeremiah Wright" (p. 167). Buell and Sigelman insinuate that racial attacks were launched by both campaigns and then go on to provide absolutely no support for this absurd claim. First, it is important to note that Obama never launched any racial attack against McCain. Buell and Sigelman offer no examples of ways in which McCain's racial identity was attacked personally or in larger context of White racial domination. Second, it is also something that is unimaginable for a racial minority candidate in a national campaign. On a basic level, no racial minority candidate could be taken seriously if he or she offended the dominant White race and only appealed to the non-White eligible voter pool. Certainly the history of candidates, such as Reverend Jesse Jackson, Congresswoman Shirley Chisholm, and Reverend Al Sharpton are poster-child examples of how difficult it is for a racial minority candidate to even be relevant beyond his/her racial grouping, let alone how well they would have done if they overtly or even subtly insulted the dominant White race. With all of this being said, it is also worthwhile to point out that, as previously discussed, McCain could have been attacked for his racial identity and history, but the Obama campaign declined to utilize these attacks options. McCain's Mississippi upbringing and his family's southern plantation roots, as well as his relatives' history of fighting for the Confederacy, could have been fertile ground to at least question McCain about his racial views and attitudes. Even more astonishing was the fact that McCain openly and unapologetically defended his use of the term "Gooks" based on his experience of fighting in the Vietnam war and being held as a political prisoner there for years. This story barely made a one-day national media splash, and it never served as a sustained campaign attack for how insensitive McCain was toward Asian Americans and/or racial minorities. Instead of exploring of these points, Buell and Sigelman followed the same path as much of the media, and they focused on Reverend Wright as the singular, racial lightning rod for the 2008 campaign:

> An apostle of Black Liberation theology, Wright laced his sermons with shouts of "God damn America!" and the "the U.S. of K.K.K.A." Videos of his most inflammatory homilies—including his declaration that 9/11 was divine retribution for America's racism—aired on newscasts and otherwise seeped into the public

domain. His railings gave Hillary Clinton an opening to attack Obama during the Democratic primaries. Whether Obama was present when Wright held forth in this manner remained unclear. Obama eventually repudiated Wright yet remained vulnerable to Republican attacks in the fall (Buell, Jr. & Sigelman, 2008).

Buell and Sigelman further entrench this problematic racial discourse by suggesting that McCain's decision to not attack Obama's religion, church, and pastor was a sincere effort to de-racialize the campaign issues and attacks. Not placing this discussion in the context of a history of presidential campaigns in which no other candidate's religion, church, and pastor had been attacked in the way that Obama's faith and religion had been in the 2008 election cycle makes the racial implications disappear. As previously discussed, presidents such as Jimmy Carter attended segregated churches. Never were sermons released from pastors of previous presidential candidates and given the same level of scrutiny as sermons given by Obama's pastor were in 2008. Buell and Sigelman's analysis of the 2008 election neglected key features and aspects of the primaries and general election, and that neglect is most noticeable in the area of how race and racism influenced and dominated these campaigns.

Another example of the way Buell and Sigelman pursue this theme of "dual racial" attacks and neglect of the most pertinent racial dynamics can be seen in their discussion of the daily campaign grind. Buell and Sigelman start by once again suggesting that Obama and McCain are simply having a racial spat and that it is a tit-for-tat affair: "At the same time, the McCain campaign hit back hard whenever Democratic attackers played the race card" (p. 59). Buell and Sigelman then add, "The most memorable such exchange began October 11, when Congressman John Lewis of Georgia, a hero of the civil rights struggle, strongly objected to the tone of the McCain and Palin rallies," and "upset by responses of 'Kill him!' and 'Off with his head!' to attacks on Obama at McCain and Palin rallies, Lewis accused the Republican ticket of 'sowing the seeds of hatred and division' a la George C. Wallace." (p. 59). Buell and Sigelman (2009) then directly use a quotation from Lewis to solidify their point, "'As public figures with the power to influence and persuade,' Lewis contended, 'Senator McCain and Gov. Palin are playing with fire, and, if they are not careful, that fire will consume us all'" (p. 59).

Buell and Sigelman conclude with these observations and an unsettling analysis:

> McCain by all accounts was deeply hurt by these allegations, and he responded with denunciation of them as "shocking and beyond pale." McCain also demanded that Obama repudiate Lewis's remarks. The Obama campaign issued an assurance that "Senator Obama does not believe that John McCain or his policy criticism are in any way comparable to George Wallace of his segregationist policies." Still, the statement concluded, Lewis had been right to condemn 'hateful rhetoric' at McCain-Palin rallies. When McCain raised the issue again at the final debate, Obama reiterated the gist of his campaign statement (p. 59).

What Buell and Sigelman did not seem to appreciate was the fact that the racial animosity and vitriol against Obama had reached such an alarming, fever-pitch level that Lewis felt a need to intervene. Lewis is not just a "hero of the civil rights struggle," he is someone who literally gave blood on the Edmund Pettis Bridge when he got his head beat in by White vigilantes and police officers. The significance of this intervention is greatly diminished by suggesting that it was merely the Obama campaign "playing the race card." Lewis was one of the few people still living who could honestly attest to what it meant to be a victim of White mob violence from the 1960s, and he had unique insight to what can lead to and trigger this type of violence. To suggest that Lewis objecting to Palin and McCain rallies where participants were screaming racial slurs and calling for the death of Obama was part of an Obama-campaign or partisan attack on McCain truly misses the way in which the entire 2008 primaries and general elections were infused with race and had reached a crescendo by the time Palin joined the McCain campaign. Buell and Sigelman even concede this point when they present contradictory insights. On the one hand, Buell and Sigelman state that, "Obama's race appeared to matter little in the polls," but on the other hand, they claim, "it excited bigots all over the country" and the "Secret Service began protecting Obama earlier than any other presidential candidate in history" (p. 234). If no other person or organization was clear about the potential threat that the McCain campaign posed for Obama and our national health, at least the Secret Service recognized these racial dynamics. On a basic level, if you have a candidate who is being presented as a monkey with a noose around its head, then that is going to be the candidate who is a much easier target and a more likely one for people to act out their hatred toward in a lethal way. This understanding of the danger for Obama that the McCain campaign posed was revealed by the Secret Service security decision, and it was an understanding of the situation that was not too different than what Lewis's stated concerns were. It was not just a matter of "excited bigots" that Buell and Sigelman incorrectly highlight as the chief racial concern, but it was instead the overwhelmingly warm, supportive environment McCain and Palin were creating in their speeches, rallies, commercials, literature, campaign surrogates, and campaign slogans for millions of Whites to embrace and act out on their racial fears and animosity. The names and death threats Buell and Sigelman reference are just the tip of this racial iceberg. The fact that so many people were openly engaged in this behavior and so supportive of the McCain campaign is what needs more scrutiny. Buell and Sigelman's work does not properly address critical questions, such as: *Why was Obama singled out for this type of deeply personal and offensive attacks unlike any other presidential candidate? Why were overt and subtle racist material and language the basis of so many of these attacks? What is the lingering impact of so many White citizens using racist language and material to attack the presidential candidate who eventually wins the election? Does this racism carry more hurtful, unforgiving, and complicated baggage than any other form or style of negative campaigning?*

From this backdrop a case for a more critical review of the methodological and theoretical work done on negative campaigning can be discussed. Even though the work of Buell and Sigelman remains the specific focus of this review, their work is emblematic of the larger field of negative campaigning, and these questions and critiques could be applied to the work of the vast majority of scholars that work within this area. Buell and Sigelman did not have the appropriate analytical tools and framework to be able to detect and evaluate race and racism in presidential campaigns. Within the specific definitional terrain that Buell and Sigelman stake out, it is possible to raise questions about what material is neglected and/or misunderstood as reiterated now. Whereas it might make a lot of sense to make a distinction between, on the one hand, "wild mudslinging" and, on the other hand, "accurate" and "fair" negative campaigning, race fundamentally changes this dynamitic. The "truth" of what candidate Obama did or not do was not as relevant as the fact that he received a certain type of scrutiny and attacks from both Democratic and Republican party candidates. Part of the lingering damage of these attacks went well beyond the logic of negative campaigning (e.g., Skaperdas-Grofman model), and it became clear that Subtle and Overt racism developed a life of its own. Obama, like the vast majority of other presidential candidates in 2008, could very well be born in the United States, a "true" patriot, and not friends with domestic terrorists, but these factual points made little difference in how he was treated. One could even argue that most of the attacks on Obama were "wild mudslinging" that was "unfair" and "inaccurate" and that they were completely ineffectual in the political realm. From the vantage point of Feagin, Weber, Thornton, Omi, and Winant, these attacks could also be considered entirely predictable and par for the course for the way race and racism operate in the U.S. An analysis of the way in which these racist attacks leveled at Obama moved beyond traditional negative campaigning and moved more into the analytical framework of race and racism will be presented from the standpoint of Wise's work.

RACIAL FRAMING

These attacks have clear identifiable racial components to them, and they can be directly linked to the forms of race and racism that Weber, Omi, Winant, and Feagin had previously described. This is also ultimately a small sample of the racial assault that was directed at Obama during the primary and the general elections of 2008. These examples clearly substantiate the fact that Obama encountered a racial assault during these two election cycles and that the attacks went well beyond traditional negative campaign tactics. An argument can be made for this assault not just having an impact on Obama's campaign and governing style but also on the national racial discourse that these attacks fed into and nurtured. One way to frame the use and the impact of these racial assaults can be seen through the work of Tim Wise. His work provides an insightful link between the various points of how and why these racial attacks were generated and what they were able to accomplish.

Tim Wise's use of the conceptual terms Racism 1.0 and Racism 2.0 provides a way to address the question of the relevancy and the significance of the racist attacks on Obama (Wise, 2009). Wise suggests that contrary to popular opinion, "the 2008 presidential election may not have been a contest in which racism was vying against anti-racism, so much as one in which two different types of racism were competing for predominance" (p. 34). This framework begins to challenge the assumption that race and racism could not have been significant in the 2008 national elections because a Black man, Obama, clearly won the elections. Wise then illustrates the way in which race and racism could have an impact in the election but not just simply from the standpoint of who won the election or how effectively an informal or a formal racist tactic was utilized.

Wise does this by first defining Racism 1.0 and by suggesting that this most abrasive, overt form of racism was not used: "On the one hand was old-fashioned bigotry, or Racism 1.0, which could have caused enough whites to vote against Obama for racial reasons as to have ensured his defeat" (p. 17). Wise presents a similar historical frame of reference utilized by Feagin, Weber, Omi and Winant to substantiate his definition of

Racism 1.0. Wise makes references to racial murder, lynchings and riots as examples of overt forms racism that support his definition of Racism 1.0. Wise then moves on to suggest that Racism 2.0 was the preferred form of attack during the 2008 election cycle. Wise makes this point based on the following observation: "On the other hand, however, was Racism 2.0—a far less easily recognized type—which could allow him to win the presidency, but only because of his ability to ease white fears and transcend his still-problematic blackness, biracial though it may be" (p. 24). Wise then concludes that Racism 1.0 might have been vanquished in this election, but Racism 2.0. was powerfully in play during and after the election. Through Wise's work it is possible to see how the racial attacks Obama encountered did not impede his ability to win the primary and general elections, but they were still effective and substantial. In particular, the way in which these racist attacks continued to have an impact on Obama's governing style and the way in which his opposition engaged him will be covered in the next chapter. Suffice to say, an argument could be advanced that the national appetite for overt and subtle forms of racism has dwindled, and these forms of racism do not represent effective and useful national campaign tools. The examples of overt racism that were previously presented suggest that even though they were produced with a national audience in mind, their impact on the primary and general elections was marginal at best. Even the subtle forms of racist attack that were utilized could also be placed in the category of ineffectual and limited utility.

What Wise then presents is how this previous discussion of Race 1.0 and Race 2.0 could be misconstrued as "racial successes" or "progress." Wise goes on to suggest that what is most relevant for understanding the current state of affairs for race and the Obama campaign and presidency can be summed up in two questions: "Rather than ask what Obama's success means in terms of race and racism in the United States in the twenty-first century, the better question may be what doesn't his success mean for those things?" and "What does it not tell us about how far we've come and how far we still have to go?" (p. 24). In answering these questions, Wise makes an invaluable point about how the Obama campaign and presidency have interfaced with the current racial discourse. This point can be understood as articulated by Wise when he declares that even while many Whites could accept and support a Black president, a significant portion of the White population may not support a Black president based on traditional Racism 1.0 grounds, and this part of the campaign was missed by the mainstream media. This sets the stage for an argument to be made about how the effectiveness and utility of the racist attacks did not result in an ultimate victory in the elections of 2008. These racist attacks, though, have contributed to the coarsening of the national racial discourse in some novel and insidious ways. The way Obama's opponents launched formal and informal racial attacks against him not only had an impact in the narrow realm of negative campaigning, but also contributed to and helped reinforce the type of 2.0 racial discourse Wise so eloquently depicts in his work. Wise's work leads to this inevitable conclusion about race and racism and Obama: "If some whites are willing to vote for a person of color, but only to the extent they are able to view that person as racially unthreatening, as different from 'regular' black people, as some-how less than truly black, or as having 'transcended race' (a term used with regularity to describe Obama over the past few years), then white racism remains quite real, quite powerful, and quite operative in the life of the nation" (p. 78). This racial framing allows one to move past the overly simplistic conclusion that Obama's victory was a victory for the anti-racist forces and that it ushered in a "post-racial" period. Through Wise's fram-ing the negative racist attacks can now be understood as contributing factors for a racial discourse (Race 2.0) that is not as crude and overt as past racism (Race 1.0) but just as potent in terms of determining the life chances for millions of racial minorities. It has also been instrumental in maintaining very narrow boundaries for racial minorities to be able to succeed and be held in high regard by the dominant society. At the same time, it is also very clear that social, cultural, and economic boundaries are being erected that exclude the vast majority of minorities from being considered eligible for social, political, and economic societal "goodies." These dynamics are especially true for racial minorities seeking certain powerful and prestigious positions.

It is now worthwhile to return to the previous examples of racial attack and present a way in which these attacks can be understood from the vantage point of Wise's work. The Overt racial attacks (Obama image placed on waffle boxes with a similar expression to an Aunt Jemima character, Obama's image on fake money with the caption: "Obama Bucks" and a picture of watermelon and a bucket of fried chicken in the background, an Obama image of him as an "Arab with a turban" on a three-dollar bill, Obama's image on a "Curious George" shirt with the slogan: "Obama '08" and a button suggesting that the White House will need a name change if Obama were elected) and the Subtle racial attacks (Obama's Hawaiian birth certificate providing the basis to question his citizenship, challenging his patriotism because of the absence of a flag lapel pin, attacks on his religious faith, his pastor, and church membership in Trinity United Church of Christ, and his full birth name: Barack Hussein Obama) all contributed to the formation and maintenance of the type of racial dynamics Wise has described. It could be argued that the real success of these attacks did not come in the form of election victories but in the reconstituting of destructive racial dynamics that could allow a racial minority to assume the highest position in the land, while leaving the overall racial dynamics for the vast majority of the non-White community firmly in place. These crude and insidious presentations of Obama were partially so ineffective because of the fact that they did not fit the actual person they were attempting to ridicule and demean. As Wise suggests, Obama was the "exceptional" Black man, and this included an Ivy League education, White mother, and unassuming demeanor. Senators Joe Biden and Harry Reid both pointed out how "articulate" and "smart" Obama was, and the implied assumptions of their analysis rested on an understanding of Obama being remarkably better than other racial minorities (Balz, 2007; Zeleny, 2010). This meant that even if these racial attacks were understood as attempts to racialize Obama and move his campaign into the irrelevant racial margins of our society, this effort completely failed. This effort did have an impact on Obama as a candidate, as well as a lingering impact on how the racial discourse in our society operates and functions on a daily basis. Unlike previous campaigns of African American candidates for president, Reverend Jesse Jackson, Reverend Al Sharpton, Congresswoman Shirley Chisholm, and Angela Davis, Obama's campaign could not be placed in the box of a Black candidate and/or a candidate promoting a Black agenda. To the extent that this was true and the racial attacks directed at him could not stick, then Obama could move to the level of relevant and viable national candidate.

The racial framing that Wise offers is critical in understanding how and why Obama was able to succeed as a presidential candidate and why these racial dynamics continued to haunt his presidency. The two questions from Wise's work that were discussed earlier can now be revisited from a slightly different angle. ("The better question may be what doesn't his success mean for those things? What does it not tell us about how far we've come, and how far we still have to go?") If the argument is going to be made that the Obama election did not significantly improve race relations, yet he had to overcome potent Overt and Subtle forms of racism to achieve these election victories, then how can these seemingly contradictory trends be reconciled? Wise describes how this new form of racism (Racism 2.0) is just as devastating as the old form of racism (Racism 1.0), and he provides specific examples from the arena of public policy. This area of the impact of these racial dynamics on the Obama administration will be addressed in the next chapter. The way "campaign Obama" had to be transformed into a non-racial, non-threating, and acceptable political alternative carried over into the President Obama who was very limited by White Nationalist discourse and structure that has historically dominated the way the executive branch has operated. The way this White Nationalism influenced Obama's campaign and governing style can be seen as the logical extension of not just the way in which Wise presents race, but also Feagin, Weber, Dill, Omi, and Winant. In the next section a discussion of White Nationalism in the executive office and public policy will be critically reviewed from the standpoint of what was demanded of a Black candidate at first, and then as a president.

As I close this discussion of White Nationalism—in which I have attempted to illustrate that race has been a central determinant in shaping important public policies—I suggest that this work may contribute to the settled proposition in the field of political science that ideology has an impact upon public policy (Walters, 2003).

WHITE NATIONALISM AND PUBLIC POLICY FOR THE OBAMA ADMINISTRATION

The history of presidents in the United States has not revealed a static history of customs and traditions. As suggested by even the terms traditional- and modern-era presidents, there have been substantial changes to not just the type of office holders but also the path taken for gaining entrance into this office. The key components of the modern era do not just include the way in which Roosevelt successfully won the presidency four consecutive times and became one of the most powerful heads of the executive Office, with an expanded professional staff, but also include the way in which this period began to reflect the massive and fundamental shifts in technology and communication that have dramatically changed the presidency and the way society operates. These changes coexist with the social, political, and economic trends that have stretched and molded what is commonly referred to as the modern era. To the extent these changes can be accurately captured by scholars studying specific aspects of past and current presidents or specific political campaigns, they can become a highly contested and debated matter. This is particularly true when race and racism are included in the discussion of these general or specific topics related to the presidency. One way to move forward with a specific discussion of negative political campaigning and the impact it has not just on the executive branch as an institution but on the specific presidency of Obama is to use Ron Walters' work on the executive branch and race.

Attention will now be devoted to how federal-level politics continues to be ensnarled in a type of White Nationalism and how the federal government plays a critical role in the maintenance and operation of this White

Nationalism. To understand how our federal government operates in a racialized context, the work of Ron Walters (2003) on White Nationalism will be utilized. Quite often those scholars that provide expertise on the executive branch do not provide a detailed analysis of the way in which race and racism operate in this realm. Michael Genovese's (2001) and James Pfifner's (2011) work provide excellent examples of traditional academic work on the executive branch that neglects the potency and significance of race and racism in the executive office. Other scholars analyze the way race and racism operate in society but do not provide a traditional academic analysis and understanding of the executive branch (Weber, 2001; Thornton Dill, 2009; Feagin, 2000; Omi & Winant, 1996; Williams, 1992; Bell, 2008; Fishman, 2013).

Walters' work provides an invaluable and unique link between traditional political scientific examinations of the executive branch and race-centered scholarship and identity-based scholarship. Walters not only provides a detailed and potent analysis of how the executive branch operates within a Constitutional framework and how social customs and traditions play a role in the daily operation of this branch of government, but he also illustrates how this segment of government has historically been grounded in racist practices and policies.

The case Walters consistently makes throughout the body of his work for how our national government operates within a White Nationalist framework is not only compelling, but his analysis can also provide an insightful way to understand the racist attacks leveled at Obama. Including an analysis of the way in which the executive branch has operated within a racial framework historically can lead to key insights into how and why Obama received racist attacks before he was elected to the office of presidency, and why he continued to be subjected to these racist assaults. This line of inquiry will also create the space for specific questions about the scope and nature of African American participation in politics and political engagement to be reviewed. Questions about the larger issues involving African American oppression and how some forms of this oppression are directly connected to the formal, and informal, federal political apparatus can also be addressed. This is an area that traditional political science and social science research has failed to address, and it also helps to focus on specific work that has been done on White Nationalism within the parameters of the executive branch. (Genovese, 2001; Pfiffner, 2011; Buell & Sigelman, 2008).

Unlike the work of traditional social sciences scholars, such as Buell and Sigelman, Walters' work utilizes a specific White Nationalist filter to be able to track and account for the way in which presidents win elections, utilize political clout, and pursue public policy matters. When Walters' work on White Nationalism is applied to this analysis of the racial attacks leveled at Obama, a specific evaluation of the way in which a White audience was expected to understand these attacks and to be receptive to these types of racial assaults can be developed. A clear political advantage can be identified here for a White audience, and these attacks present a White audience with an opportunity to utilize these attacks in a politically advantageous "racialized" way. This logic is a radical departure from the previously discussed Skaperdas-Grofman model that was solely based on what was needed for a particular candidate to win an election. Placed within a racial context in which African Americans have been historically oppressed and the executive office has advanced and promoted the cause of White Nationalism, questions about how Obama was able to achieve an electoral victory and how he has governed take on a different level of meaning and significance. Walters' work on White Nationalism covers the post-civil rights Democratic and Republican presidencies from 1976 to 2000. His work relies heavily on a critique of not just who the office holders were and how they were elected, but mostly on the actual public policy positions they advocated and what policy initiatives they were successful in implementing. This work clearly predates the Obama presidency, and it is within this framework that the Obama presidential phenomenon can be situated and properly evaluated. Walters' analytical framework provides an excellent vantage point to compare with the scholars who work in the area of negative campaigning and legacies of past presidencies, as well as those who work specifically on race or identity politics in general.

WHITE NATIONALISM AS AN EXPLANATION

Walters describes a type of White Nationalism that is built upon and constructed on White power that is not only reflected in national politics and public policies, but in the day-to-day social conditions of White people. Walters defines White Nationalism as "a sociopolitical phenomenon [that] is based on substantial evidence which suggests the proposition that if a race is dominant to the extent that it controls the government of the state—defined as the authoritative institution of decision making—it is able to utilize those institutions and the policy outcomes they produce as instruments through which it also structures its racial interest" (Walters, 2003). This definition is based on an understanding of race that is similar to the work that has been done by other experts in the field of race (Feagin, 2000; Wise, 2009; Omi & Winant, 1996), as well as scholars concerned with intersectionality and identity politics (Weber, 2001; Thornton Dill, 2009). Walters carves out his specific piece of this larger matrix of anti-racist work being done by focusing his attention on the way White Nationalism as an ideology interfaces with national government structure and policy production.

To make this case, Walters starts by showing how White Nationalism has historically operated in the U.S. and continues to function today. Walters builds upon and utilizes many of the key tenets of previous works on how race and racism operate in our society. In particular, Walters places the roots of White Nationalism within the context of the history of Western Europe and follows the same historical grounding that Feagin, Weber, Wise, Omi and Winant utilized: "The idea of nationalism, with its corresponding conception of the nation-state, seems to have first emerged in Western Europe," and it "found its fullest flower in England and France, where 'just as the king had required undivided allegiance in the days of royal supremacy, so managers of the sovereign nation-state of the nineteenth century expected not only loyalty to the state but also identification with the language, culture and mores of those who controlled it'" (Walters, 2003, p. 44). This history connects with the type of historical orientation for race and racism in the United States that

Feagin presents in his work. Feagin (2000) specifically draws attention to the history of the Constitution: "The year is 1787, the place Philadelphia, fifty-five men are meeting in the summer's heat to write a constitution for what will be called the 'first democratic nation'" (p. 18). From this historical grounding Feagin offers more crucial insights about the founders who "create(d) a document so radical in breaking from the monarchy and feudal institutions that it will be condemned and attacked in numerous European countries" (p. 18). Feagin also explicitly states, "These determined radicals are all men of European origin, and most are well-off by the standards of their day" and "Significantly, at least 40 percent have been or are slave-owners, and a significant proportion of the others profit as merchants, shippers, lawyers, and bankers from the trade in slaves, commerce in slave-produced agricultural products, or supplying provisions to slave-holders and slave-traders" (p. 18). Feagin's work relies heavily on historical evidence to establish the way in which the current racial discourse is inexorably linked to United States and European history. These insights, combined with Walters' description of the formal history of White Nationalism, begin to present a clear picture of how a particular type of White Nationalism developed and became embedded within the executive branch. This focus on historical development of political institutions also begins to give shape and form to how race and racism continue to operate in society. It is not just a matter of a racist comment or even a racist policy, but it is also a specific structure and way of operating that is utilized by the federal government. It is a phenomenon that other scholars have observed, monitored, and documented (Weber, 2001; Feagin, 2000; Omi & Winant, 1996).

Walters presents a specific understanding of race that is not simply based on society being stratified along racial lines and the White/European race continuing to be the dominant racial group, but also on the understanding that the continuation of this White/European conception of political, social, and economic relations operates as the accepted norm. The White Nationalist historical roots Feagin describes connect directly to the way in which Walters describes the influence of the Western European conceptualization of political power and how it was transferred to the new American colonies. Walters describes this ongoing phenomenon in the following way: "The White majority is proceeding to concentrate economic and social power within its own group, using its control over the political institutions of the state to punish presumptive enemies" (Walters, 2003, p. 124). Walters and Feagin dip into this same historical well when they provide the same grounding for White Nationalism based on its specific theoretical Western European roots, as well as from the lived reality of the American colonies and the distinct American traditions and customs that grew out of this history. This historical analysis begins to provide a definition of White Nationalism that does not depend upon a specific politician or political party, and it begins to open a way to examine larger institutions and structures of government. This analysis moves away from the more arcane and detached approach many scholars have utilized for this subject matter in the past and begins to illustrate how these "neutral" institutions were always deeply entrenched in racial power relations and that this was part of the fabric of the society that was developed at that time.

This analysis also provides a way to examine contemporary politics from a racial prism and move away from the more simplistic explanation that is usually attributed to U.S. political culture, customs, and traditions. Walters introduces two key concepts that provide the basis for his racial analysis of contemporary policies: Convergence Politics and Policy Racism. Walters defines Convergence Politics by first establishing a racial link between the two political philosophies that are typically associated with the two major political parties in the United States, Democratic and Republican. Walters does this by describing the ideological basis of these philosophies in the following way: "What the two perspectives, one Liberal and one Conservative, have in common is that they both affirm the subordinate status of Blacks in relation to Whites as a basic value, a paradigm that, if challenged or changed, would activate both Liberals and Conservatives alike to seek to protect their status and reimpose subordination upon Blacks" (Walters, 2003, p. 38). Walters adds, "This paradigm is so powerful that it has the capacity to energize Whites to invoke common interests and come together regardless of differences of political ideology or party" (p. 38). From this vantage point Walters is then able to argue that the pendulum has swung towards the conservative side of this ideological fight, and it is has further enshrined political discourse in a White Nationalism frame. Walters describes this frame in the following the way: "The White Nationalist ideology of the current Conservative movement has driven the Democratic party to move much closer to positions held by the Republican party" (p. 39). Walters then specifically defines the term he will use to describe this phenomenon: "I will describe what might be called 'the politics of convergence' to illustrate the mechanism of racial consensus" (p. 39). Walters is then able to examine liberal and conservative ideologies, as represented by the two dominant political parties in the United States, and show how race has infused and dominated the way that these ideologies have contributed to the development and implementation of public policy. To do this Walters also reviews three specific public-policy issues that have a direct impact on African Americans and other non-White racial communities: poverty programs, the criminal-justice system, and public education. In his very thoughtful and detailed analysis of these areas, the overarching thesis of White Nationalism is persuasively presented.

The second key term Walters offers to buttress his argument for the way that White Nationalism interfaces with the executive branch is the term Policy Racism. From the standpoint of the federal government, real public policy "winners" and "losers" can be identified and evaluated along racial lines. Walters claims, "The targets of this punishment have been Black, Hispanic and other non-White communities" (Walters, 2003, p. 7). In his chapters about the poverty programs, the criminal-justice system, and education, Walters provides a brilliant case for why African Americans have been the "losers" in these public-policy areas historically and why this continues to be true. In his chapters about the dominant political parties and political players, Walters also presents an exceptional analysis of how in the public policy areas he covers (anti-poverty programs, the criminal-justice system, and education) there is little difference between the public-policy positions of the two dominant parties. Walters explains why this results in a Policy Racism and how this form of racism is grounded in White privilege and non-White neglect and harm, but presented as the end result of a public-policy process that ultimately benefits the national interest: "Yet White decision makers routinely rely solely on their non-experiential opinions to pass laws that determine the quality of life in the Black community," and "This raises the questions of whether the policy is formulated from a sense of the general 'national interest' from a perceived fear of harm to White self-interest—whether this fear is experiential, theoretical, or based on the likelihood of a threat" (p. 52). White domination of all of the political levers of power on a federal level has real-life consequences for racial minorities. This can be seen in the development and production of a Policy Racism that can be observed and evaluated, and this is a critical component of the way in which White Nationalism operates in the United States. (Walters, 2003).

The basis of the methodological criteria to establish and evaluate White Nationalism that Walters proposes includes three areas: the racial representation of elected government officeholders, the policy that is generated and voted on by government institutions, and the actual impact that these policies have on Whites and non-Whites. To advance this argument Walters also introduces an understanding of what Black (non-White) interests are and how these interests have become are a critical component of this White Nationalism and executive branch puzzle. Walters first makes the point about the existence of and the legitimacy of Black (non-White) interest: "Despite the fact that the deprecatory term 'identity politics' is used with reference to the discourse and activities which flow from minority group mobilization, the underlying White racial interests in objective majoritarian politics has drawn little attention from analysts, except in the case of defensive references to 'reverse racism'" (p. 53). Even though Walters acknowledges that "all Blacks don't think alike," he does want to argue that "there does exist a Black mainstream opinion on most important issues that constitute dominant consensus of the group" (p. 53). From this basis Walters can then make the case that these Black interests are neglected and hurt in the production and implementation of public policy. Concepts such as Convergence Politics and Policy Racism capture this neglect and harm. Walters' methodological criteria and concepts come together then to not only offer an explanation of current and past public-policy development and production from the vantage point of the executive office but also explain why in the area of White Nationalism so little has changed. By including the three methodological points (the racial representation of elected government officeholders. the policy that is generated and voted on by government institutions, and the actual impact that these policies have on Whites and non-Whites), it is easy to understand how a shift or a fundamental change in one of these areas would not immediately correlate to any substantial improvement in public policy from the standpoint of Black (non-White) interest. In other words, a change in the race of the office holders or even a change in those who participate in elections would not necessarily have an impact on the policy produced and advocated, for that plays a vital role in the day-to-day lives of millions of racial minorities.

This leads to an analysis of the Obama presidency and another way to appreciate the curiosity and excitement about the first Black president. From the standpoint of these criteria, it can be concluded that the work done on making federally elected officials more racially diverse must be connected to the actual policy positions that are retained, modified, or abolished and what impact these policy changes have (or do not have) on communities of color. The Obama presidency can be connected to Walters' work, and the limitations of a Black presidency become more apparent through the type of analytical lens Walters develops. A purely cosmetic change in the racial political representation that is not linked to the public-policy development and implementation that has an impact on millions of racial minorities would not have any type of positive, lasting impact on the racial dynamics and discourse in the U.S. Put simply, a change in the race of elected officials in the executive, legislative, or judicial branch of the federal government would not necessarily result in a positive change in the social conditions millions of racial minorities struggle with on a daily basis. From this backdrop the Obama presidency will be evaluated in the next section.

RACIAL ASSAULT AND THE OBAMA PRESIDENCY

Based on Walters' insights in the areas of White Nationalism, public policy and the executive branch, one could have correctly anticipated a great deal of resistance to Obama running for president and an Obama presidency. From the simple standpoint of a Black man attempting to obtain the most powerful position in the world, it would make a lot of sense for there to be an overt and subtle White Nationalist reaction to this pursuit. Walters' work allows someone to view the previously covered material on Subtle and Overt racial attacks directed at Obama during his presidential campaign and after his presidential campaign victory as not just individual examples of personal assault or part of normal negative campaigning but as attacks which are part of a systematic and historically structured White Nationalist racial discourse. The real power associated with the executive office is well understood by the majority White audience. Political elections are heavily "staged" and meticulously choreographed affairs, and it is in that sense that the abundance of these "isolated" and "individual" racist attacks can be understood not as some random and accidental events. Some of the candidates Obama ran against in the Democratic primary and the general election attempted to use basic White fears to their advantage, and this contributed to an environment in which Subtle and Overt racist attacks could be launched against Obama. Moving beyond the overt hostility held by some Whites toward any Black person being elected to the office of presidency, there was also the crude racial calculation made by some of the candidates to exploit any potential racial fears held by White voters with regards to what a Black president might mean for the most prestigious and powerful position in the country, as well as what it might mean for national culture and traditions.

To the extent that these racial attacks could have successfully kept Obama out of the White House, the previous discussion of the "isolated" production and use of racist images can be understood within the more simple (Racism 1.0) racial framework of exclusion and assault (Wise, 2009). These racial attacks did not succeed, and the more insidious racial goal (Racism 2.0) could be identified as the door opening for only a certain type of Black presence (Wise, 2009). Once Obama was elected, it could be further argued that these attacks continued to apply pressure on the Obama administration, and they served as a reminder of the limited space he might be afforded to govern. In other words, the Overt racial attacks became part of a clear message delivered to African Americans about what stepping out of place might mean for real or imagined policy positions (Wise, 2009). What better way to keep Black people in their place than by reminding them of their inferior historical place through what the dominant media presented as innocent, non-racial and isolated incidents. Overt racial attacks, such as the waffle boxes, "Obama bucks," "Obama food stamps," "re-naming the White House," and "Curious George shirts" were not obscure reminders of what has been America's collective imagined space for Black people historically and arguably the space that some Whites believe Black people should continue to reside in. It is also a view of what public- and professional-space Black people should aspire to be in and operate in. Once outside of this "safe" public space, Black representation and perception becomes par for the course of what is considered threatening and what must be feared. An actual African American running for president represents the pinnacle of this fear and provides an insightful explanation of why so much overt and subtle racist material was produced to attack Obama.

In the area of Subtle Racism were numerous examples of negative campaigning (e.g., United States citizenship, patriotism, Christian faith and church pastor, and birth name) in which race and racism seeped into the attacks launched at Obama. Besides the more crude and rudimentary racial images and characterizations of Obama, more subtle forms of racism appeared in the campaign. Most of these attacks were either directly or indirectly connected to questioning and attacking Obama's citizenship, patriotism, birth name, and religious faith. As previously discussed, people who questioned Obama's U.S. citizenship are referred to as "Birthers," and some of these people have been a part of what has been called the

"Birther Movement." Some of the more prominent attacks on his patriotism have been directed at his unwillingness to wear a flag lapel pin, his attendance at a "terrorist training" madrassa as part of his primary education in Indonesia, and his association with Bill Ayers, who was a former member of the Weather Underground. Attacks on Obama's religious faith and practice focused on his church, Trinity United Church of Christ, and pastor, Reverend Jeremiah Wright. Of course, Obama's middle name, Hussein, received a great deal of scrutiny and ridicule. All of these lines of attack were not only predictable, but arguably provided the exact support needed to substantiate the potency of Walters' White Nationalism theory. Put simply, if Obama was not attacked in these areas, and if the emphasis of the attacks on Obama were on his public-policy positions, then some version of the "post-racial" thesis could be more persuasively presented. All of these examples support the criteria Walters established for the existence of White Nationalism within the executive branch. In similar fashion as the overt racial attacks, the subtle racial attacks also occupied the space of attempting to block candidate Obama from obtaining the presidency and then shifted after the election to move into the realm of stifling any potential meaningful public-policy agenda and implementation of that agenda.

It is not surprising then that these racial assaults persisted even after Obama's second presidential election and continued with Overt and Subtle racial language and symbols being used. Despite the fact that the rationale that this was part of the typical election-cycle hyperbole might be used to explain some of the racist discourse, the continuity of this racial assault suggests that a larger racial discourse must be providing part of the basis for what enabled these attacks to continue unabated. Even after two elections, the attacks against Obama did not subside or return to a more traditional questioning and challenging of policy positions and legislation. The assaults on Obama continued to incorporate and capitalize on insidious Subtle and Overt racial language, symbols, and messages. It is also important to note that these racial assaults were not limited to one political party or campaign period. Obama encountered just as many challenges to his racial identity during the

Democratic primary as he did during the general election. In particular, during the time that Obama was running against, at that time, Senator Hillary Rodham Clinton, demeaning pictures of Obama in African garb were "mysteriously" released. The Clinton campaign also released a political commercial questioning whether or not Obama could be trusted as Commander-in-Chief to answer the Red (emergency) Phone in the middle of the night, and President Bill Clinton declared that the state of North Carolina was not a significant state election to win because even Reverend Jackson had won that state. All of these episodes have direct or indirect racial overtones, and all of them highlighted and drew attention to Obama's racial identity. Having a visual image of Obama in African garb reinforced the erroneous view of Obama as a foreigner or a non-citizen; the red phone advertisements played upon the White fears of whether or not a Black man could truly be trusted to protect and serve America in its darkest moments, and President Clinton's comments about North Carolina literally "Blackened" North Carolina into a state of irrelevance by suggesting that any Black man could and should win that state. Walters' central thesis rests upon the fact that there is very little difference between public policies developed by the two major political parties for racial minorities. It should not be surprising that one Democrat would use race attacks against another Democrat in a primary election. Democrats and Republicans are both likely to use a White racial advantage when it serves their respective purposes.

To examine why this continued to be the case and what some of the implications of these ongoing racial assaults might be, I would like to turn back to Walters' work. The meaning and significance of these race-based challenges to Obama's policies and presidency are primarily based on an audience's ability to glean a particular type of racial meaning and significance from these attacks, not just their ability to find character flaws or weaknesses in his politics or the public policies he pursues. To the extent that these racial attacks are used and considered successful, they can be thought of as a clear indicator of the state of American race relations and, in particular, the way in which current racial discourse can continue to dominate people's lives.

OBAMA, RACIAL ASSAULT, AND PUBLIC POLICY

The Obama administration's decisions on what public policy to advocate and how to implement these policy positions can be understood as inextricably linked to the way in which these "innocent," "non-racist intent" and "isolated incidents" have been reported by the mainstream press. A discussion of these attacks can shed light on to what extent they were partially or completely racist in motivation and intent, but equally important, the impact that these attacks had on Obama's governing style, in particular, in what ways public policy coming from the executive branch could be developed and advocated for during the Obama administration after the campaign racial attacks and then during the continual onslaught of racial offenses. The assumed significance and novelty of the racial attacks on Obama will be analyzed from this vantage point. Even from the standpoint of the accepted logic of Obama being the first Black president and the first president to encounter racial attacks, the implications of these attacks are not clear in terms of the development and advocacy of public policy. It has been quite common for people inside and outside of academia to not only accept that Obama encountered significant personal and political attacks but also to accept that Obama struggled with vicious and unprecedented racial attacks on his presidency. These attacks have rarely been properly analyzed and addressed from the standpoint of public-policy development and advocacy by the executive branch. Questions then, about the nature and the scope of the attacks on Obama should first be addressed within an historical context of attacks leveled at previous presidents and then, second, they should be critically reviewed from the standpoint of race and racism. Once the attacks are placed within the context of those leveled at previous presidents who received non-racial attacks and once the impact of these attacks has been reviewed, then a more meaningful evaluation of the attacks on Obama in terms of public-policy development and advocacy can be developed.

After Obama was elected the first time, White opposition to his presidency expanded to include not just his presence in office but to the actual challenge he might represent to White privilege. It is possible to argue that to the extent Obama was able to keep these White policy benefits in place, he then could counteract some of the White hostility to his power. By the same token, to the extent that Obama was and continues to be viewed as either a symbolic or substantial challenges to these White policy benefits, one could expect a significant backlash to the Obama presidency. This can begin to explain why once Obama moved into the White House, the Subtle and Overt racial attacks leveled at Obama did not subside, and he had no "honeymoon" period or a period in which granting of respect was accorded to him by nature of the office he occupied. This opposition was not just based on public policies, political parties, or even a clash of personalities. To illustrate this point, one striking case of a national racial uproar will be reviewed, and another case of a public policy debate that was racialized around African American reparations will be examined, as well as a discussion of how Obama's first significant policy victory received a racist backlash.

A great deal of hostility and raw anger was directed toward Obama when he spoke in favor of his friend, Dr. Henry Louis Gates, and critically of the way that police in Cambridge treated Gates (Ogletree, 2010). The severe public reaction could be understood as based on racial animosity (Ogletree, 2010). Gates had the highly public misfortunate of not being able to quickly unlock the door of his house. He sought help from his driver, and neighbors called police to investigate this suspicious behavior. Not surprisingly, Obama spoke in favor of a professor with whom he was friendly. What was extraordinary was the way the police officer, Sargent James Crowley, who arrested Gates for having trouble trying to enter his own house, was not only perceived as an "equal" victim to Gates in this incident but garnered national support and sympathy. Somehow the thought of a Black president calling a White police officer's actions stupid in this one case was too much for the racial consciousness of this country, and the national police union actually threatened to march on Washington, D.C. Even the basic educational moment that Obama shared with the nation about how Black men are unfairly treated everyday by authority figures did not seem to be received and understood by the public. The potential for discussions about the criminal justice system and the way current public policies contribute to the racial bias in this system was completely lost. This incident becomes critical because it was not a radical or even moderate shift in our criminal justice public policy that Obama was advocating or had presented to the American public. Obama was simply trying to offer his opinion about an unfortunate event, but this event had a loaded racial backdrop attached to it. This incident was an all-too-common occurrence for Black men who are "mistakenly" stopped, frisked, harassed, and sometimes even arrested by police officers. Obama stepped into this racial hornets' nest, and the White backlash was immediate and intense. Obama was not only forced to backtrack from his comments, but he was also pushed into a setting up a meeting with Sargent Crawley and Dr. Gates as a way to diffuse the situation. This also allowed Obama to attempt to refocus national attention onto the national health care debate. One could glean from this incident that the image of an African American president presented as anti-police would have been politically damaging and that Obama's administration attempt to diffuse the situation was in part, or totally, based on assuaging the fears of the majority White electorate that could turn against the president based solely on his handling of this incident.

It is worth noting that the Gates-Crowley incident "interrupted" the national health care debate, and this provides a second example of the way in which a public policy debate became racialized. The health care debate could be presented as an example of a discussion that started at the exact opposite end of the racial discourse spectrum. Unlike Obama's comments about the Gates' police incident that could easily be construed in a racialized context, the health care debate was not, first and foremost, a racially charged public policy debate. On the most rudimentary level, it was supposed to be based on the most pure of political intentions: An earnest attempt to improve the living conditions of those with the least through developing more affordable and accessible health care options. Given the modest reforms proposed by the Obama administration for health care, it should have been shocking and a complete surprise that conservative critics of this health care reform referred to it as "reparations for African Americans" (Klein, 2010). At first glance, Rush Limbaugh's and

Glenn Beck's comments could easily be dismissed as the most extreme and racist of the conservative talk show hosts and irrelevant for any serious discussion of public policy. It would be very easy to argue that the intent of Obama and other advocates of health care reform was not based on providing reparations for African Americans or based on direct benefit to any other racial minority. A more nuanced and careful reading of these comments, though, and one that is accompanied by Walters' analysis of White Nationalism and the executive branch, could specifically link these race-based comments to the proposed changes in the health care system to the previously discussed racial attacks leveled at President Obama. With the onslaught of racist attacks on Obama soon after he declared his candidacy in 2007 for the Presidency and the steady drumbeat of these attacks continuing after the first presidential election in 2008, the groundwork had been established for an effective overt and subtle racialized discourse to be utilized to negate any type of modest policy agenda or even an agenda that would specifically support racial minority communities.

Another example of a racial assault on Obama that had direct links to the production and implementation of public policy was the stimulus package. This was literally the first major accomplishment and fight for the Obama administration, and it was also brazenly mocked and ridiculed in an overtly racist fashion by the *New York Post* (Fig. 5.1):

Fig. 5.1.

This racial attack on Obama once again went beyond the personal bounds of simple insult (Obama presented as one dumb, dead monkey) and into the realm of racial discourse (history of Black people presented as animal-like and specifically as monkeys). The way these attacks intertwine with a larger discourse does mean that whole racial groups are being subjected to the hurt, and in that sense, these attacks do real harm to racial discourse. It is also important to note that these attacks, by the same token, help to support and maintain a form of racial privilege for Whites. It is not a past White president that has been presented as a dead monkey after his first major legislative victory, and all previous White presidents did not have to endure a form of racial attack that was connected to a history of overt oppression. This attack provided Obama with another clear message about how the norms and customs that have been previously discussed for past presidential elections would apply to his presidency. These same norms and customs that were ruptured by racist attacks leveled at him as a presidential candidate continued to not apply to him even after he made transition into the formal office of the presidency. This meant that advocacy and support for public policy could come with great peril, and the potential racial cost and damage would have to be factored into public policy work. In other words, once Obama took a stand on a particular issue, that position could then be "Blackened" for public consumption and understanding. The substance of Obama's position or the meaning of his advocacy was not relevant. What was important is the fact that a Black man supported this position, and this Black man can be seen through the racial filters applied to him and his work. Who, then, wanted to side with the dead monkey on a policy debate? Who would want to accept as legitimate policy something produced by an animal that the New York City police had to put down? This is not to suggest complete paralysis for the first Black president, but this serves as acknowledgement and an appreciation of the formidable Overt and Subtle racial barriers and obstacles that Obama struggled with and worked through.

PRESIDENT OBAMA'S OWN RACIAL CALL AND RESPONSE

Another way to assess and evaluate the racial temperature is to review the exact moments when President Obama has introduced race in the most overt fashion. Unlike the previous examples where race was interjected, typically by his opponents, it is critical to also observe the ways in which Obama has attempted to discuss race and what might be considered the moments that most closely represented his own views of race and racism. Three moments where Obama discusses race arguably present not just his own views but could be considered progressive and visionary views of race. The first is his previously mentioned "race speech" in Philadelphia during the time of the Democratic primary. Even though this speech was produced in response to attacks on Obama's former pastor, Rev. Jeremiah Wright, key components of this speech contain identifiable racial narrative that Obama attempts to communicate. This narrative entails the following three elements: 1) a very careful inclusion of the dominant narrative version of U.S. history buttressed by the inclusion of African American history and insights, 2) personal grounding that includes White and Black relatives, and 3) an idealistic multi-racial and multi-ethnic vision for our society.

Obama's Philadelphia speech included specific historical references. In his 2008 speech, Obama declares, "The document they produced was eventually signed but ultimately unfinished," and adds that the Constitution "was stained by this nation's original sin of slavery, a question that divided the colonies and brought the convention to a stalemate until the founders chose to allow the slave trade to continue for at least twenty more years and to leave any final resolution to future generations" (Obama, 2004, p. 1).

From this point, it is easy for Obama to move into the second area that requires him to pivot into his own personal life. With regards to this area one can find Obama's unique heritage becoming the centerpiece of his campaign, as well as his presidency.

I am the son of a black man from Kenya and a white woman from Kansas. I was raised with the help of a white grandfather who survived a Depression to serve in Patton's Army during World War II and a white grandmother who worked on a bomber assembly line at Fort Leavenworth while he was overseas. I've gone to some of the best schools in America and lived in one of the world's poorest nations. I am married to a black American who carries within her the blood of slaves and slaveowners—an inheritance we pass on to our two precious daughters. I have brothers, sisters, nieces, nephews, uncles and cousins of every race and every hue scattered across three continents, and for as long as I live, I will never forget that in no other country on Earth is my story even possible (Obama, 2004, p. 1).

Finally Obama suggests the path forward has to move down a road of healing of past historical wounds and recognition of what all share. Obama expresses this message of hope and healing in the following way:

That is one option. Or, at this moment, in this election, we can come together and say, "Not this time." This time we want to talk about the crumbling schools that are stealing the future of black children and white children and Asian children and Hispanic children and Native American children. This time we want to reject the cynicism that tells us that these kids can't learn, that those kids who don't look like us are somebody else's problem. The children of America are not those kids, they are our kids, and we will not let them fall behind in a 21st century economy. Not this time (Obama, 2004, p. 1).

These key elements can be traced back to his speech at the Democratic Convention in 2004 that substantially raised his national spotlight. In that speech the refrain of red and blue states and what is done and known in these states is typically what is most recognized. The overall message of what Americans value and treasure should supersede what is associated with red Republican states and blue Democratic states, and this notion of a shared ethos is most significant for Americans collectively as a people. This specific racial message utilizes these rhetorical, as well as substantial, themes. At the start of his quest to become president, to the extent that Obama embodied this racial vision and was able to effectively communicate this message he was not only politically successful but was also able to develop a very popular and potent political brand. This approach carried over into race and racism, and when Obama ventured into the swamp of racial discourse for American politics, it was based on a notion of shared American identity. This shared American identity needed to include real sources of historical and contemporary pain for all American children. This would appear to be a brilliant and simple strategy for Obama as the candidate and as the first African American president. Given the previously documented pitfalls of other African Americans that ran for president, a purposeful attempt to not be locked in the box of a "Black candidate" or a candidate for "Black America" was essential for the success of the Obama campaign and presidency.

This approach was tested often once candidate Obama shifted to President Obama. The tension between the shared vision of American identity and racial uplift on the one hand and ongoing racial turmoil, strife, and oppression on the other hand reared its ugly head on multiple occasions. The first notable occasion was early on in the Obama presidency when he spoke in support of his friend Dr. Henry Louis Gates after Gates was arrested by the Cambridge police. It is worth reviewing this previously discussed incident in the context of Obama's exact comments from the press conference that started the national firestorm.

Since these comments have quite often been misconstrued as an overall attack on the specific officer who arrested Gates and/or the entire Cambridge police officer, it is important to examine the way in which

Obama very carefully and thoughtfully described this incident. Obama presented this story in the following manner:

> They're reporting—the police are doing what they should. There's a call, they go investigate what happens. My understanding is at that point Professor Gates is already in his house. The police officer comes in, I'm sure there's some exchange of words, but my understanding is, is that Professor Gates then shows his ID to show that this is his house. And at that point, he gets arrested for disorderly conduct—charges which are later dropped. Now, I don't know, not having been there and not seeing all the facts, what role race played in that, but I think it's fair to say, number one, any of us would be pretty angry; number two, that the Cambridge Police acted stupidly in arresting somebody when there was already proof that they were in their own home; and number three, what I think we know separate and apart from this incident is that there is a long history in this country of African Americans and Latinos being stopped by law enforcement disproportionately. That's just a fact (Transcript: Obama's News Conference, p. 1).

With these off-the-cuff comments, one can see the similar themes and points of emphasis as Obama's prepared speech on race in Philadelphia, as well as some key points of departure. First, he is hesitant to personally provide any racial analysis, but he acknowledges a racialized history that must be considered as the appropriate context for an incident involving a White police officer and an African American man. Second, unlike his previous race speech, he does provide a moral judgment for the specific police actions that resulted in what he believed to be an unwarranted arrest. This incident is based on the harm inflicted on an African American male without the immediate space available for acknowledgement of

RACE, RACISM, AND THE EXECUTIVE BRANCH | 161

the dominant racial group's source of pain, too. Only later, once Obama received criticism from police organizations and unions, did he not only strategically retreat from his comments, but he also attempted to acknowledge White suffering. This was done through the awkward and hastily organized "Beer Summit" with Gates and Sargent Crowley. This staged event gave the optics of an unfortunate incident between two co-equals and left the impression that to the extent that racial harm was inflicted on anyone during this incident, it was shared equally. This becomes the critical filter through which the Obama presidency has encountered and processed racial events. When the racial caldron has bubbled over and moved to the level of presidential response, it has typically been within the context of severe racial pain and trauma.

The next example of this type of incident and presidential response came with the tragic death of an African American teenager named Trayvon Martin. Trayvon Martin was shot and killed on February 26, 2012 in Sanford, Florida. The shooter was George Zimmerman, a self-proclaimed neighborhood watch coordinator for the gated community that Martin was returning home to the night of the fatal altercation. This left an undeniable mark on the public conscience because of the fact that Martin was not only another young, unarmed African American teen that was killed, but that Zimmerman was a civilian, and he was not even arrested after this shooting. Zimmerman's substantial claim of self-defense was not only based on the formal Florida state Stand Your Ground law being included in the judge's instructions for the jurors to consider but also the unstated shared fear of a Black man that was explicitly and implicitly stated by Zimmerman, his public defenders, and his attorney. Martin's hoody, his suspicious behavior, and his unwillingness to properly answer Zimmerman's questions became the base for why it was reasonable for Zimmerman to follow, approach, and eventually use lethal force during their altercation. Even when Zimmerman was given specific instructions to stand down and wait for the police, his open defiance of these instructions from the 911 operator were not enough to change the inevitable course toward an acquittal of Zimmerman against manslaughter charges. By the time the verdict was announced, a national campaign was in full support of

Martin along with a more low-profile campaign in support of Zimmerman. A racial divide developed and was constructed along the lines of one side believing that an innocent Black boy was killed again, and this fed into the deep resentment and mistrust on the part of, first and foremost, African Americans and other racial minorities that continue to be the victims of these racialized incidents, and, on the other side, those, especially from the dominant racial standpoint, who believed Zimmerman was sincerely attempting to protect his community and that this neighborhood had been a target of many previous crimes.

Within this backdrop Obama attempted to interject a presidential claim on this issue and navigate through all of the potential racial perspectives that existed for the public at that point. As with the Gates incident, the risk for Obama was that if his message was received as biased in favor of Martin and he identified too closely with Black suffering, then it would not be effective or useful for a significant part of the American public. This could be construed as racial bias and favoritism and could present the opening for an intense White racial backlash. For the popular American psyche, the thought of an African American president not only acknowledging Black pain and bringing attention to this suffering, but the fact that a president could be motivated by this suffering and utilize his presidential power to address the racial harm inflicted on a racial minority was beyond pale. On the other hand, the fact Obama is perceived as and treated as Black in society also meant that it would be difficult for him to address these national racial episodes without personal grounding. The path that Obama created in his prepared remarks on both occasions attempted to address these various points of racial tension.

> You know, when Trayvon Martin was first shot, I said that this could have been my son. Another way of saying that is Trayvon Martin could have been me 35 years ago. And when you think about why, in the African American community at least, there's a lot of pain around what happened here, I think it's important to recognize that the African American community

is looking at this issue through a set of experiences
and a history that doesn't go away (Remarks by the
President on Trayvon Martin, p. 2).

From this vantage point Obama creates the space to not only talk about
race in a personal way and to identify publicly as an African American,
but he also creates the space to be able to address African American
experience for the national audience from an insider position that has the
potential to raise racial consciousness. Obama finishes his comments with
this final potent observation:

> There are very few African American men in this coun-
> try who haven't had the experience of being followed
> when they were shopping in a department store. That
> includes me. There are very few African American
> men who haven't had the experience of walking
> across the street and hearing the locks click on the
> doors of cars. That happened to me—at least before
> I was a senator. There are very few African Americans
> who haven't had the experience of getting on an
> elevator and a woman clutching her purse nervously
> and holding her breath until she had a chance to get
> off. That happens often (Remarks by the President on
> Trayvon Martin, p. 2).

With the Martin speech delivered after the jury in Florida acquitted
Zimmerman of all charges, Obama proceeded to articulate a position
that had not only showed proper deference for our legal system, but also
acknowledged the deeply divided racial reaction to the jury's verdict.
The key point for Obama was to make sure that the racial minorities' perspective was not dismissed or considered irrelevant after the acquittal of
Zimmerman. Obama once again offered personal experience as an entry
point into a collective Black understanding of race and racism but also
as a way for the country to move forward. Given the substantial attacks

leveled at Martin in terms of drug use (trace amounts of marijuana found in his blood after he was killed) and violence (previous history of fights and a picture of a gun), this speech had many potential pitfalls. The most immediate danger for Obama was that he could be perceived as supporting a "street thug." These accusations represent the type of mythic Black "street thug" that Middle America fears most and that would certainly damage any national political figure and could be politically lethal for the first African American male president.

With that being said, it is worth noting the exact words selected to convey Obama's post-Zimmerman acquittal message. In particular, Obama braces his audience for his comments by stating, "I don't want to exaggerate this, but those sets of experiences inform how the African American community interprets what happened one night in Florida," and "it's inescapable for people to bring those experiences to bear" (Remarks by the President on Trayvon Martin, p. 2). Obama moves on to suggest that, "The African American community is also knowledgeable that there is a history of racial disparities in the application of our criminal laws—everything from the death penalty to enforcement of our drug laws" (Remarks by the President on Trayvon Martin, p. 2). Lastly, Obama drives home his point about identity politics and how this informs our experiences, as well as the development of our political views and beliefs: "And that ends up having an impact in terms of how people interpret the case" (Remarks by the President on Trayvon Martin, p. 2).

It is not surprising that this speech received high marks from many African American political, social, and religious leaders and was met with a great deal of general approval by racial minorities. Obama provided insights into lives of African American men that are rarely given national attention, and to the extent that this message was distributed through national and social media, many were heartened to see this portrayal of Black lives and Obama's personal connection to these lives. It is also worth noting that some people took exception to this speech and criticized it along these exact racial lines. One example of this critique could be seen in the title of Lee Habeeb's article in *National Review Online*: "A White Person's Reaction to Obama's Trayvon Martin Speech." (Habeeb, 2013).

The basis of Habeeb's critique is that Obama neglected to identify with Zimmerman and that because Obama is both Black and White, he should be responsible for articulating both sides of this conflict. This, not surprisingly, raises the previously mentioned points about Obama's first major race speech in Philadelphia and the apparent high level of political success he was able to achieve with this speech. For an African American president to speak about race without acknowledging White experience has been solidified as unacceptable and out of bounds and that the level of success that one can gain from moving into racial terrain must be measured by the ability to articulate this shared American identity and experience. The three key areas that Obama covered in his race speech in Philadelphia included 1) a very careful inclusion of the dominant narrative version of U.S. history buttressed by the inclusion of African American history and insights, 2) personal grounding that includes White and Black relatives, and 3) an idealistic multi-racial and multi-ethnic vision for society but were most noticeably devoid of the component of the dominant narrative (and experience) in this country. This begs the question of whether or not the Philadelphia race speech is the only model that can be used by a president, White or non-White, and if the national racial tragedy is based on the loss of Black (or racial minority) life, then what is the most appropriate and valuable approach that should be utilized by the executive branch? Would "equal" representation of Zimmerman's life by Obama balance the scales of racial justice in our society and would that type of speech ensure that U.S. society would be less likely to have similar incidents in the future? This shift in Obama's public approach to race for Martin received the predictable rebuke from some quarters, and it highlights the prescribed boundaries for a president to be able to address race and racism. These boundaries are more tightly monitored and controlled when the president is African American and has been consistently attacked on racial grounds and has received intense racial push back on a personal level, as well as on a level of public address and policy advocacy.

The last speech from Obama that presents significant insights into his own views of race and racism in America, as well as the political and social minefield embedded in this discourse, is the one that launched his

"My Brother's Keeper" initiative. Unlike the previous examples of Obama's speeches that attempt to address specific racial wounds, My Brother's Keeper represented public policy in its most pure form. This policy initiative was not based on substantial federal dollars being allocated or a large, new bureaucracy, but it was based on the following principles:

1   "Ensuring all children enter school cognitively, physically, socially and emotionally ready

2   Ensuring all children read at grade level by 3rd grade

3   Ensuring all youth graduate from high school

4   Ensuring all youth complete post-secondary education or training

5   Ensuring all youth out of school are employed

6   Ensuring all youth remain safe from violent crime" (The White House, My Brother's Keeper, 2014)

On this non-racial level of success for "all youth," one can also recognize this program as bi-partisan and non-ideological. On another level, this program was also very much presented in the public domain as grounded in race. The specific goal for My Brother's Keeper is to support Black and Brown youth (The White House, My Brother's Keeper, 2014). This can also be seen in Obama's remarks about this program. Obama begins his comments by describing a visit to Hyde Park Academy in Chicago, only one mile away from where he used to live. The school has a student body that is 99% African American.

From this backdrop one can begin to appreciate the selection of this school for a visit and how the story of his visit becomes relevant for the introduction of Obama's My Brother's Keeper initiative. Obama offers this story in the following way:

> During my visit, they're in a circle, and I sat down
> in the circle, and we went around, led by their

counselor, and guys talked about their lives, talked about their stories. They talked about what they were struggling with, and how they were trying to do the right thing, and how sometimes they didn't always do the right thing. And when it was my turn, I explained to them that when I was their age, I was a lot like them. I didn't have a dad in the house, and I was angry about it, even though I didn't necessarily realize it at the time. I made bad choices. I got high without always thinking about the harm that it could do. I didn't always take school as seriously as I should have. I made excuses. Sometimes I sold myself short. And I remember when I was saying this—Christian, you may remember this—after I was finished, the guy sitting next to me said, "Are you talking about you?" (Laughter.) I said, yes. And the point was I could see myself in these young men. And the only difference is that I grew up in an environment that was a little bit more forgiving, so when I made a mistake, the consequences were not as severe. I had people who encouraged me—not just my mom and grandparents, but wonderful teachers and community leaders—and they'd push me to work hard and study hard and make the most of myself. And if I didn't listen, they said it again. And if I didn't listen, they said it a third time. And they would give me second chances and third chances. They never gave up on me, and so I didn't give up on myself (The White House, My Brother's Keeper, 2014).

Obama establishes a personal grounding again that clearly resonates with the youth he was meeting, as well as the large audience of Black consumers of his message. To the extent that an initiative like My Brother's Keeper can be effective and valuable, the targeted communities must embrace and have faith in this initiative. It is also vital that not only is a certain level of community buy-in needed, but the specific areas that will be addressed by this initiative, as well as the goals of the program, must also be clearly articulated. Obama (2014) presents these components of the initiative in the following two-step manner:

> If you're African American, there's about a one-in-two chance you grow up without a father in your house—one in two. If you're Latino, you have about a one-in-four chance. We know that boys who grow up without a father are more likely to be poor, more likely to underperform in school. As a black student, you are far less likely than a white student to be able to read proficiently by the time you are in 4th grade. By the time you reach high school, you're far more likely to have been suspended or expelled. There's a higher chance you end up in the criminal justice system, and a far higher chance that you are the victim of a violent crime. Fewer young black and Latino men participate in the labor force compared to young white men. And all of this translates into higher unemployment rates and poverty rates as adults (The White House, My Brother's Keeper, 2014).

From this vantage point of the real racial harm for Black and Brown youth, Obama then is able to shift into the way in which solutions for these social, political, and economic problems can appear impossible to reach. Whereas there may be "bipartisan" and "non-ideological" agreement about these statistics, the way to move out of this racial morass becomes the divisive and controversial area.

Obama provides the following path to break through the traditional roadblocks for policy in these areas, starting with recognition of how and why these race-based problems remain so entrenched in society. To make this point Obama states that:

The worst part is we've become numb to these statistics. We're not surprised by them. We take them as the norm. We just assume this is an inevitable part of American life, instead of the outrage that it is. (Applause.) That's how we think about it. It's like a cultural backdrop for us—in movies and television. We just assume, of course, it's going to be like that. But these statistics should break our hearts, and they should compel us to act (The White House, My Brother's Keeper, 2014).

The final component of his speech that is noteworthy is the description of the "action" that Obama alludes to as being necessary for the parts of the racial quagmire he has highlighted. Obama offers these thoughts:

So we all have a job to do. And we can do it together— black and white, urban and rural, Democrat and Republican. So often, the issues facing boys and young men of color get caught up in long-running ideological arguments about race and class, and crime and poverty, the role of government, partisan politics. We've all heard those arguments before. But the urgency of the situation requires us to move past some of those old arguments and focus on getting something done and focusing on what works. It doesn't mean the arguments are unimportant; it just means that they can't paralyze us. And there's enough goodwill and enough overlap and agreement that we should be able to go ahead and get some things done, without resolving everything about our history or our future (The White House, My Brother's Keeper, 2014).

This lands Obama in the very familiar terrain of his major race speech in Philadelphia, as well as his first national speech at the Democratic party convention. The overarching theme is that bipartisan and non-ideological solutions for the racial problems that plague society are needed and can be achieved. With the launch of this new presidential initiative it is too early to offer any substantial analysis of the success of this program and the impact it has had on intended communities. It could end up being based on more "smoke and mirrors" and not enough support could be provided to the Black and Brown youth that are most in need of the type of services and programs this initiative claims to offer. One can also pose the question of what is available for any president to do in terms of race and racism and whether or not in the limited scope of presidential options if My Brother's Keeper is the "best" option. Is there a way for a president to address the substantial and structural changes that many believe are needed for the racial stratification that still dominates society? This understanding of society has provided the basis for the critiques of the Obama administration that were previously discussed in terms of leftist and race-based politics. The other side of the political equation that I have suggested, and is buttressed by the work of scholars such as Walters, is that the public policy considerations that overtly address the areas of racial minority oppression run the risk of being rejected by the dominant White majority population. If what is needed from the legislative and/or the executive branch for addressing the racial problems that plague society is considered impossible to introduce politically and advocate, then what is the more "palatable" package that could be offered politically, and would this potentially watered down and less potent option be worth pursing, and how one would assess and evaluate this, by definition, "compromised" political solution? The lack of significant racial blowback to this presidential initiative suggests that it was presented in an effective fashion and that significant racial openings are available for the executive branch. What will be closely monitored and evaluated now is exactly how the social, political, and economic statistics Obama referenced are addressed by this specific initiative, as well as by his policies overall. Since the economic downturn in 2008 and the overt racial disparity in how hard the recession hit the Black and Brown community, even more intense political and ideological focus will be drawn to these areas and the solutions being developed and advocated by government officials from the local to the national level.

CONCLUSION

Walters has written extensively about race, power relations, and the federal government. One of the clear themes that can be identified in this work is the way in which White Nationalism operates within the executive branch and how this White Nationalism has been historically apparent in Democratic and Republican presidential administrations. The precise and succinct way Walters presents White Nationalism, and how he ties it directly to how the executive branch operates in the U.S. through terms such as Convergence Politics and Policy Racism allows for his work to interconnect with traditional social science work, as well as with scholarly work done on race and racism.

The thread that ties these diverse areas together is the racism that is not just utilized on a personal level (presentation and critiques of the president) and his policies (criminal justice reform and health care), but to the overall failure to produce any effective federal government programs and support for racial minority communities. One of the most significant dilemmas Walters' work highlights is the failure of Democratic and Republican presidents to develop and advocate for policy that will improve the lives of African Americans and other racial minorities. When this analysis is applied to President Obama, and it is granted that one of the three methodological stool legs of Walters' work (racial representation of office holders) is effectively addressed, it is also abundantly clear that two of the legs are still neglected (the majority White electorate and policy advocacy and development). If it is understood that some semblance of a three-legged stool must come together to not only be able to challenge personal racial assaults but also to effectively address the substantial policies inadequacies, then comments from Rush Limbaugh and Glenn Beck can be taken much more seriously. Their comments tap into the deep well of racial animosity that is still very potent and can still limit public policy development and advocacy work done by the executive branch. It could even be argued that an African American president presents a racial liability for public policy and that a "traditional" White Democrat would enjoy greater space for public policy and electoral success.

The federal government's public policy decisions and implementation of these decisions are a reflection of society's broader understanding and acceptance of a larger racial discourse that allows for this federal government work to move forward. Through his specific analysis of education, welfare, and criminal justice policies, Walters argues that the federal government has failed to properly support and nourish the Black community. He also claims that there has been active public support, in terms of percentage of majority White voters and the elected officials they have voted into office, for the direction in which the federal government has moved. Walters suggests that the stranglehold of White power is kept in place by the racial makeup of elected officials, the policies they support, and the racial impact of these policies. In significant racially-tinged policy areas, such as affirmative action and welfare, Walters finds that little policy difference between the two major political parties (Republicans and Democrats) and little difference in views on these issues for the White members of these political parties. The intensity of attacks on Obama do not then reflect a radical departure in policy positions for the Democratic or Republican party on policy issues, such as affirmative action or welfare, but clearly represent a pronounced discomfort with his racial identity. The intended, or unintended, consequence of this hostility could have been not just the downfall of Obama (as a one-term president) but could also have been the more alarming demise of a change in policies that directly apply to large portions of the African American population (such as welfare and affirmative action). Put another way, if a Black president causes such great discomfort for a certain portion of the White community in the U.S., then what is the likelihood that the deeply embedded and structured racism that continues to plague society can ever be addressed? Is it possible that racial representation is a lower threshold barrier to meet, and producing public policies that are more supportive and nurturing of non-White communities is a higher bar of achievement?

IMAGE CREDIT

- Fig. 5.1: from New York Post. Copyright © by NYP Holdings, Inc.

CONCLUSION

THE PROVERBIAL PUBLIC POLICY RHETORIC MEETS THE REAL POTHOLE IN THE ROAD

The rhetoric that government has failed leads to the question of whom it has failed as well as to another question, one that is seldom asked: Would Blacks have been better off without the publicly sponsored social programs of the 1960s? The generally received wisdom—that all the Great Society programs have failed Blacks, other minorities and women—is demonstrably false. Perhaps another question would illuminate this further: If nothing worked, then where did the Black middle class come from?

Walters, 2003

INTRODUCTION

OBAMA PRESIDENCY AND THE RACIAL ASSAULT HISTORY OF ATTACKS ON PRESIDENTS

When attempting to wrestle with what exactly is unique about our first African American presidency the easy answers rarely provide much insight. In attempting to establish Obama's racial identity as being a significant component of his presidency I analyzed the historical legacy of previous presidents. It was through the filter of attacks on previous occupants of the White House that I first attempted to illustrate the novel nature of the Obama presidency. The historical legacy of African Americans in the United States is most identifiable from the standpoint of extreme forms of oppression, starting with slavery and moving into Jim Crow. The legacy of this oppression should have been a noticeable component of the Obama presidency, and it should have manifested in a distinct form from previous presidents. By reviewing the traditions and style of attacks utilized against candidates running for president, as well as those against sitting presidents, it became clear that the racial assaults Obama encountered stand out. Through the traditional and modern era of politics there were significant shifts in the tenor and veracity of attacks leveled against candidates in campaigns and for office holders, but none of these attacks carried the marked weight and burden of racialized assaults. Whether it was the very personal attacks or even the absolute carpet-bombing style of attacks utilized, these forms and traditions of attacks never reached the level of the attacks directed at Obama.

THE SCIENCE OF NEGATIVE CAMPAIGNING

To substantiate this observation, the specific work of scholars developed for the study of negative campaigning for presidential office was critically reviewed. The work of Buell, Jr. and Sigelman provided an example of contemporary scholarship for negative campaigning, and it represented the myriad of challenges that can be seen as part of this field of study. Even with the very careful steps with which these scholars started and the appropriate areas they addressed, it became very apparent that there were inherent weaknesses for this field of study, and the Obama campaigns and presidency exacerbated these weaknesses. If for methodology the established messengers of negative campaigning (the candidate, his/her surrogates, party structure) and acceptable mediums to evaluate (television, radio, internet, billboards, newspapers) could be agreed upon, this would leave large areas of contentious theoretical terrain open for debate. Buell, Jr. and Sigelman's attempts to narrow their focus and to examine the specific presidential campaigns from 1968 to 2008 and to use the *New York Times* as the primary source for negative campaigning in presidential campaigns offered, ultimately, very little light they could shed on Obama's campaigns and presidency. In fact, they reached the startling conclusion that the 2008 presidential election was the least negative based on the theoretical matrix they developed for interpreting 40 years of presidential negative campaigning. What is most remarkable was the fact that a methodological approach could be developed for identifying and tracking negative campaigning in presidential elections, along with an accompanying theoretical model that could be used to explain these results, but none of this work could lead to any better understanding or appreciation of the fundamental dynamics in the election of the first African American president. Put simply, if it could be offered that the 2008 election was the most overtly racist presidential election that has ever occurred, then how could these racial dynamics not be properly identified and covered by the methodological and theoretical tools most closely associated with this field of studying presidential elections? To ask this question was to presuppose that this was the most racist presidential election, and it is this key element of my own analysis that I explored next.

FROM RUN, JESSE, RUN
TO NO DRAMA OBAMA

Part of the missing link in the work done on past presidential elections was the sheer novelty of an African American running for president for a major party and who was considered a viable candidate. To the extent that no precedent existed for racial minorities being at this level, the corresponding lack of coverage and interest from within academia and outside of academia made sense. Why identify and cover racial dynamics in presidential campaigns if they do not exist in any significant and meaningful fashion? If all of the major candidates for the two dominant political parties are White, then what more significant and meaningful racial dynamics can one ascertain from this typical race? One could even ask why would it be assumed that the simple elevation of an African American candidate to the level of prominent, credible presidential candidate would change these racial dynamics?

To address these questions, it was important to bring the discussion of attack campaigns in presidential elections back to the historical reality of other racial minorities that have run for president. The one candidate that can be seen as most comparable and relevant to Obama's campaigns (and his eventual success) was Reverend Jesse Jackson's presidential campaigns in 1984 and 1988. Even though Rev. Jackson did not win the Democratic party nomination in either of these campaigns, he clearly encountered various forms of racial discrimination. One level of racism he encountered was the sheer shock to the American political system that his campaign represented. What was remarkable about the type of criticisms Rev. Jackson's campaign endured is that they were usually couched in political terms. He was labeled as too leftist for the country and that the U.S. could never elect a radical candidate like Rev. Jackson. In hindsight, it can be easily understood that many of the same criticisms Obama encountered carried the same racial undertone, but that they were directed a substantially different political message and philosophy. Apparently an African American running with more middle-of-the-road, centrist politics still represented a dangerous shock to the system, and Obama's campaign was vociferously opposed by camps within the Democratic party, as well as the Republican party. The attacks leveled at Rev. Jackson not only help to flesh out the way in which Obama was attacked but also the degree of difficulty for social scientists to identify and understand the nature of these attacks. Whereas some of these attacks may appear at first blush to be generic, run-of-the mill negative campaigns, their utilization and their targeting of African American candidates becomes suspect. The overarching element of these attacks can be seen in the questioning of would these attacks be used against a White candidate and would this line of attack have as much of an impact on a White candidate?

SAMPLE OF RACIST ATTACKS

These questions lead to inevitable analysis of the actual racist attacks and the response to the attacks leveled at Obama. What distinguished Obama's presidential run and eventual victory were the racial attacks directed at him and his campaign. Unlike any other presidential campaign, the racism in the campaign was not limited to racist policy positions, campaigning, or tactics and strategies. The overt and subtle attacks launched against Obama started with the reality of his racial identity, and that in and of itself was the nature of the critique of him. The sample of racist attacks I provided illustrated the unique way in which race was used in the 2008 primary and general election. Whether it was the overt or subtle attacks, racism was effectively utilized, though not in terms of his ability to win the Democratic party nomination or the general election. Even though it could be argued that these types of racist attacks were used against candidates such as Reverend Jesse Jackson, Congresswoman Shirley Chisholm, and Reverend Al Sharpton, and that these attacks had a detrimental impact on their campaigns, the impact of the attacks against Obama was more noticeable with regards to the lingering and ongoing impact they had on his ability to govern and to develop and implement policy. The point was not just that Obama had to position himself as a post-racial candidate and express race-neutral views to succeed, but that he still encountered a racial assault on par with any of the other African American candidates that were presented by the media as "race-based" candidates. The racist attacks then continued against Obama well after both of his election victories in 2008, and as I documented, they continued to operate around some key principles. In particular, the rise of the "Birther Movement" that specifically challenged his U.S. birth certificate and the attacks on Obama that stemmed from his lack of "Americanness" represented a unique and pernicious racial assault on a presidential candidate and sitting president. In the area of overt racism, the images and messages directed toward Obama not only fixated on his African American racial identity but also frequently were placed in the context of racist representations of African Americans that have historically been common in popular culture. The subtle racist attacks ultimately accomplished the same goal as the overt and were just as potent and as effective. While not relying on easily identifiable racist tropes, the subtle racist attacks represented probes and challenges of his Christian faith, American citizenship, and patriotism. At first blush, these attacks could appear to be innocuous and common political campaign rhetoric. Placed in the context of how other candidates were treated with similar political faults and liabilities and understood as part of an overall racist assault, these attacks could be understood as having an implicit racist message and consequences.

RACE, RACISM, AND THE EXECUTIVE BRANCH

To be able to appreciate and understand the attacks on this level, the way in which race and racism operate in U.S. society would need to be to incorporated into the analysis. Moving from the point of establishing and accepting that these attacks are racist to the point of assessing the impact of these attacks can be done from the standpoint of the history of African Americans in the U.S., as well as from the vantage point of the specific role of the executive branch in this history. An examination of these attacks from the vantage point of African American history can be done first and then the added element of the federal government, with specific attention given to the executive branch, can be examined last. The work of scholars such as Weber, Feagin, Omi and Winant provide a way to understand how these attacks connect to the way in which society is dominated by a harmful racial discourse. The oppression of African Americans has historically relied on not just material inequality but also cultural and psychological deprivation and assault. The attacks on Obama carry to this realm and do not just exist on the plane of typical executive branch discourse. It was not just simply a Democratic presidential candidate who was being contested or someone who had policy positions that one disagreed with, but it was someone who was "foreign," "unpatriotic," and a "secret Muslim" that was being opposed. To this end, the subtle and overt racist attacks became acceptable tactics and strategies to utilize against the African American candidate. To maneuver past this and not become bogged down in the racial discourse of being an African American, the Obama campaign attempted to present a "race-less" candidate for a "post-racial" country. As part of this attempt to counter overt and subtle forms of historical racism, Obama's actual life story provided a perfect antidote: White biological mother, working-class upbringing, Harvard law school education, African American wife and two beautiful daughters. As noted by Wise, this personal history and the way it was presented to the American public also ended up reinforcing other very problematic components of the racial discourse. Through his use of Racism 1.0 and Racism 2.0 Wise suggests that even if it is accepted that the more crude and abrasive forms of racism are less likely to be used now and that this represents a certain level of progress, it is also true that this does not mean that all forms of racism have been extinguished. Wise suggests that Racism 2.0 can be presented through the prism of acceptable racial minorities and how they are treated and accepted by the dominant society. This argument would be applied to Obama with regards to the fact that he has the right personal characteristics for the position. Put more simplistically, Obama was not someone that could be easily categorized by using one of the more social and politically dangerous racial tropes, such as the Black radical or angry Black man. This then distinguished him from previous African American candidates such as Reverend Jackson, Reverend Sharpton, or Congresswoman Chisholm, and it also represented a consciousness effort by the Obama campaign to not suffer their political fate, too. As Wise aptly points out, Obama's level of potential success did come with very thorny racial baggage. Part of the consequence of his success was giving validity and legitimacy to the process of who decides which African Americans are acceptable for these very powerful and public positions. Wise argues that the strengthening of this dominant-society-imposed standard of acceptability for African American national candidates can adversely impact the potential pool of African Americans that could be excluded because of their lack of a personal narrative that would resonate in a safe and comforting fashion for a primarily White audience. This raises more questions about how Obama's success can reinforce some of the worst aspects of racial discourse and potentially lock out many other racial minorities from similar types of opportunities in the future.

WHITE NATIONALISM AND PUBLIC POLICY FOR THE OBAMA ADMINISTRATION

In terms of the executive branch, it is useful to understand the historical legacy of the federal government's impact on the African American community. The ways in which African Americans have been historically oppressed, as well as the specific role the federal government has played in this process, can be glossed over and not properly understood.

The significance and meaning of the founding democratic principles of the U.S. are often given great deference, and they are also included in any narrative about a successful development model being based on the extension of rights and privileges to more people. Unlike this common narrative that is based on the creation of an egalitarian and democratic form of government and posits that this governmental structure has been the cornerstone of U.S. society since the late 1700s, a more insightful counter narrative can be gleaned from the tacit and explicit support of racist policies by the federal government. This narrative, as articulated by Feagin, is based on the systematic destruction of first Native Americans and then Africans who were brought to the country as slaves. It was not just the role of the executive branch historically in the establishment and maintenance of race-based policies, such as, for Native Americans, land removal and creation of reservations, and for African Americans, slavery and Jim Crow, but it was also the process by which this power base was developed, consolidated, and became entrenched. Walters' work on White Nationalism can elucidate this process, and his work can provide a way to critically engage the historical legacy of the executive branch.

The schematic Walters provides for assessing the racial nature and operation of the executive branch relies heavily on three core components: 1) the racial makeup of the electorate, 2) the racial identity of presidential office holders, and 3) the racial impact of policy developed and advocated. To the extent that it can be established that historically the White race has been the majority of eligibility voters for presidential elections, that until 2008 only White males had been presidential office holders, and that the policy that has been developed and advocated for past presidents has favored the White race, these elements have solidified race and racism as core elements of the executive branch historically and suggest that this type of racism will be extremely difficult to challenge and successfully overcome. Walters' description of the entrenched nature of racism on the federal level connects to the way in which one can profoundly misunderstand the election of the first African American president. With or without an African American president these forms of racism will continue to exist, and these forms of racism are not merely linked to the racial identity of the occupant of the White House. These factors then become part of the racist fabric that Walters described and presented as a White Nationalism structure in theory and practice. Based on the work of Walters, it can be argued that a limited scope of public policy options and debates are currently generated and utilized by the two major political parties. What can also be gleaned from this work is how little an African American president can offer in terms of battling against the institutional forces of White Nationalism in the executive branch.

Walters describes a type of White Nationalism that is built upon and constructed to support a type of White power and privilege that is not only reflected in national politics and public policies but also in the day-to-day social conditions of how White and non-White people live. His analysis of the federal government can be utilized to understand the racial attacks on Obama before and after the elections, as well as to understand his coming to terms with how these racial attacks connect to the maintenance of a problematic racial status quo in the U.S. (Walters, 2003). This description allows for the debate about whether or not these are insignificant or significant racial assaults to be moved into a discussion of executive branch politics. This level of analysis incorporates and builds upon the work of many other race-centered and identity-based scholars. Even though it could be argued that these attacks would appear to be predictable and unavoidable from the standpoint of Walters' theoretical framework, it does not preclude doing a lot more work by scholars and activist alike. The dilemma Obama supposedly presents as the first African American president and the expectations that were attached to his presidency can be partially resolved by the analytical framework that Walters offered. On one level, the mere fact that Walters included the racial makeup of the electorate, the racial identity of the federally elected officials, and the actual public policies developed and implemented by these elected officials provides a compelling reminder of why the racial assaults have been directed at Obama and why these attacks continued to have real policy implications. The more thorny questions of how to effectively address the specific problems of White Nationalism on the executive branch level or how this work might be linked to other effective anti-racist work do not have any easy or simple answers. Walters' work provides openings for more fruitful questions to be posed and addressed from the standpoint of how the racial attacks on Obama contribute to a re-trenching of U.S. racial politics and what possible openings these attacks might provide on the level of the executive branch, as well as the day-to-day lived experience of non-Whites.

This re-framing of how to analyze the Obama administration that Walters' work on White Nationalism provides can also be useful for assessing critiques of the administration. As suggested at the beginning of this book, Obama has been intensely critiqued from when he declared his candidacy, and these criticisms only ratcheted up after he was elected. The emphasis of my work has focused on the racist attacks that have been leveled at Obama, and the perpetrators as well as the intended audience for these attacks have usually been people associated with right-wing or conservative political ideologies. In that sense, these attacks have served as a way to buttress Republican national campaigns for candidates, such as Senator McCain in 2008 and Governor Romney in 2012, but also as way to attract and build a base of White voters that would be attracted to a race-based message directed at Obama. The "success" of these racist attacks could not simply be measured by the election results, but must also be considered in how Obama's governing style and policy advocacy and implementation is evaluated. It was also important to understand how the actual racial assault, as well as the ever-present possibility of racial attacks, played a significant role in the way the Obama administration approached policy considerations and how Obama developed his own governing style. Through the work of Feagin, Wise, Weber, Omni and Winant, I attempted to lay the groundwork for the way in which race and racism continue to operate in U.S. society and that these racist attacks have to be seen in the context of an overall toxic racist climate. Despite the "failure" of these attacks to keep Obama out of office, the amount and intensity of the attacks directed at Obama was not reduced. The attacks became a staple, a constant feature, for the campaign and governing style of the first African American president.

OBAMANATION OR ABOMINATION OR JUST ANOTHER DAY IN AMERICA?

These racialized incidents became critical not simply from the standpoint of personal harm to Obama or even what offense might be taken by the larger African American community. What was most troubling was the ongoing impact these attacks had on Obama's ability to advocate for and develop policy, as well as the way he could govern. What seems to be lost in the coverage of these incidents is the way in which they nourished and relied upon a larger destructive racial discourse and that this discourse continues to wreak havoc on millions of racial minorities daily. These racial assaults then should not be presented as isolated incidents or innocent mistakes or even as a new acceptable political discourse. Whether it is the more overt or subtle forms of racism that are being utilized, all of this material is drawn from the deep well of racial discourse that has been historically developed, and it is this history and practice of racism that needs to be highlighted. If these types of attacks are allowed to persist, there is always the risk that they will intensify and increase and will also have long-term consequences well beyond negative campaigning tactics and strategies for presidential elections. The fact that most of these racial attacks have primarily come from outspoken conservative White men and that these comments are most often supported and appreciated by largely White audiences suggests that some tangible (perceived or real) White benefits can be attached to these attacks. It also means that the success of these attacks cannot simply be measured through research done on negative political campaigning or other scholarly research done on the history of past presidents. These attacks and the impact they have on race relations will consistently run the risk of being lost and not being properly assessed if they are analyzed only through the narrow prism of presidential politics and traditions.

This raises the question of who should be responsible for stopping these attacks and ensuring that they do not contribute to deteriorating racial discourse in the U.S. It is worth noting that Obama's acceptance of the dominant media's presentation of these attacks as insignificant and unworthy of substantial coverage lends credibility and support to these deceptive and harmful media practices. Obama's political calculation may very well have been based on the assumption that if he responded to the attacks and made a vigorous case for why they are racist and should not be tolerated, then he could have received negative media coverage of himself as "an angry Black man" or as simply trying to play the "race card" to his advantage. Certainly, he could have faced a significant White backlash against a Black president protesting against racial attacks directed at him, and the sympathy of this audience might have dwindled. Even if this type of shrewd political calculation (viability for a second term as president) was the motivating force for Obama and many of his supporters, it does not change his role in this racial-assault equation. The critical response to these racial assaults has been inadequate, and it can be convincingly argued that Obama shares as much responsibility for this muted response as the mainstream media or even the Republican party.

The question of responsibility becomes a fundamental point of departure in the context of what my previous work has established. If it can be persuasively argued that the typical sources of responsibility have a vested interested in denying accountability for their role in the production and maintenance of this racial discourse, then this must also be seen as part of the larger political historical struggle with race and racism in this country. Even with the added dynamic of more subdued forms of racism being more commonplace now, it has not detracted from the ultimately insidious and destructive role race continues to play in society. Part of the way that this dilemma can be identified and critically engaged is through exact critiques of the Obama administration. Instead of any attempt being made to integrate the way the Obama administration encountered and responded to subtle and overt forms of racism with how they developed and advocated for public policy, the more rudimentary and simple analysis of Obama was as just another president who was completely ineffective and/or ideologically wrong on major issues. On a certain level some significant similarities are evident between ideological critiques from the left and the right of the political spectrum. The way in which these critiques merge on the level of supporting a racial discourse through either embrace and support (right) or through denial and dismissal (left) provides another critical lens through which to view the Obama administration.

LEFT AND RIGHT POLITICAL CRITIQUES OF OBAMA

Having established the existence and relevancy of these attacks, it is important to assess what the implications of these attacks might have for future academic scholarship, as well as general public debates about the presidency. The way in which racist attacks on Obama are isolated and separated from any other part of his Presidency is a common thread that runs throughout liberal and conservative circles. This process of attempting to provide critiques of the presidency that is divorced from the lived reality of Obama, as well as the public racial attacks, is ultimately shortsighted and limits the potency of the analysis.

From the right side of the political spectrum, it is easy to identify and comprehend many of the ideological attacks that have been directed at Obama. These critiques were neatly summarized by independent critic Andrew Sullivan (2012): "The right's core case is that Obama has governed as a radical leftist attempting a 'fundamental transformation' of the American way of life. Mitt Romney accuses the president of making the recession worse, of wanting to turn America into a European welfare state, of not believing in opportunity or free enterprise, of having no understanding of the real economy, and of apologizing for America and appeasing our enemies" (p. 1). Sullivan (2012) goes on to say, "According to Romney, Obama is a mortal threat to 'the soul' of America and an empty suit who couldn't run a business, let alone a country" (p. 1). It would make political sense for conservatives to focus on the failure of Obama to provide a robust recovery from the recession, and certainly after eight years of President Bush's multiple military enterprises questions could be raised about Obama's commitment to continuing this hawkish foreign policy. These are basic red-meat areas for conservatives. What is more troubling are the attacks on Obama in which he is portrayed as "a radical leftist attempting 'fundamental transformation' of the American way of life" and "a mortal threat to the 'the soul' of America" (Sullivan, 2012). It is on this hyperbolic level that the link to a racial discourse is completely ignored and unacknowledged by conservatives. Even though within the modern presidential history these attacks have not been the sole domain of the Republican party, and they have been used against other presidential candidates and office holders, there is still no way to de-link the racial implications of these lines of attacks. When the racial attacks are primarily based on a version of fears of a Black man in the White House, then critiques that suggest that the country is at risk of a fundamental transition or the loss of its soul are the equivalent of the other side of these racist coins. These more polite political attacks that Sullivan identifies are more digestible and useful if there has already been the lower level of feeding of more overt and subtle messages to the same targeted politically conservative audience.

This facade of a more politically dignified and acceptable discourse is quite often ripped open and laid bare by some conservative politicians and pundits. It is at this point that the links between these two realms can easily be identified as part of a larger racial discourse. One example is an interview Ann Coulter had with Sean Hannity on Fox television before the 2012 general election. Coulter immediately launched into a racial narrative to explain and criticize the Obama presidency, and she began this process innocently enough with the observation that Obama might not really be leading the national polls because, "taking a look at the polls, Coulter didn't take them too seriously noting that they 'over-predict' victory for a black candidate" (Vamburkar, 2012, p. 1). Romney was not the losing in the national polls to another candidate, but he might actually have been leading in the polls because he was running against an African American man. Coulter returned to this racial logic later in the interview when the discussion moved to specific battleground states:

> After a discussion of which states, and specifically which battleground states, Romney could win tomorrow, Coulter noted that the polls essentially show the key states to be a tie—and then brought up the race factor. "You got the Bradley effect, when you have a white man running against a black man ..."
> (Vamburkar, 2012).

Even though the Bradley effect circulated within some political circles in the 2008 election, it was put to rest by the fact that Obama commanded such a substantial national election, even in states that the Bradley effect might have been noticeable and significant. The more basic problem of trying to apply the Bradley effect, which referenced a specific California-state election in which the African American mayor of Los Angeles lost two gubernatorial elections, to a national election was that it did not necessarily manifest equivalent racial dynamics or pitfalls. What is most intriguing is Coulter's constant use of race to delegitimize and invalidate commonplace political knowledge. In hindsight, it would be easy to claim that Coulter's analysis was completely inaccurate and off base, but that would not be remarkable. Advocates of losing campaigns often present the most optimistic spin to support and nourish the campaign until the bitter end. Coulter is not only mistaken in her political analysis, but the addition of her racial analysis was also completely false. Her movement then from what could be considered mainstream conservative critiques of Obama (Coulter going on to note that Obama, aside from "wrecking the economy with the stimulus, wrecking the country with Obamacare," has done nothing but campaign) to the outlandish suggestions about the Bradley effect and the inability of national polls to correctly predict the leader in the presidential election ("The polls over-predict a victory for a black candidate") was illustrative of the way race seeps into and infects the entire political discourse (Vamburkar, 2012). Vamburkar also points out that Coulter's analysis reaches a dramatic climax towards the end interview when she claims,

> "More now than ever before," Coulter replied, "Americans are afraid to say they are voting against Obama because they'll be accused of racism. That is the point by the entire NFM [Non-Fox Media]" (Vamburkar, 2012, Nov. 5).

The implied logic of this racial insight is that if Obama were not Black, a majority of the electorate would vote against him. Henceforth, the only thing propping up the Obama administration are no policies positions or legislative victories, but simply the racial fears of the majority of White voters still hold. This reverse race logic suggests that race only matters to the extent that others unfortunately and mistakenly make it an issue. For Coulter to suggest that this was the main force driving the 2012 election is to ultimately give credence and legitimacy to a racial discourse—not a racial discourse based on any facts or scientific research (nothing cited by Coulter or anyone else advocating this position), but instead on a primal level of what Whites must be feeling when they go to vote and make that fateful decision to vote for a Black man! Once again this connects to the fundamental questions about where this fear came from and specifically what made Obama such a scary Black man? Who or what makes White people think that voting against Obama will mean that they will be labeled a racist? It could be submitted (if the ground had not been laid with a regular stream of racist images and messages) that the potential of a vote for or against Obama would not have to be cast in such a racist light. The irony is also that President Obama never presented himself as a race-based candidate, and he never advocated race-based polices that could be potentially perceived as dividing races. Coulter could still be dismissed as a fringe figure on the extreme end of conservative pundits, and her entertaining work could be easily dismissed. It is important to add another layer of analysis for conservative arguments and to bring into the discussion the standard bearer for the Republican party in 2012.

In terms of mainstream conservative and Republican circles, very little distinguishes their critiques from those leveled by Coulter and pundits like her. One potent example of the way in which these two different factions of the conservative movement converge could be seen in the comments from Mitt Romney that were secretly taped and leaked to national press sources:

> There are 47 percent of the people who will vote for the president no matter what. All right, there are 47 percent who are with him, who are dependent upon government, who believe that they are victims, who believe the government has a responsibility to care for them, who believe that they are entitled to health care, to food, to housing, to you-name-it. That that's an entitlement and the government should give it to them. And they will vote for this president no matter what ... These are people who pay no income tax. My job is not to worry about those people. I'll never convince them they should take personal responsibility and care for their lives (CNN, p. 1, 2012).

Besides the obvious political faux pas of dismissing almost half of the electorate as irrelevant for himself (and the national political party he supposedly represented), the racial institutions and language packed in this comment are noteworthy. Romney made these comments at a political fundraiser for wealthy contributors without the expectation that his comments would end up being the lead news story for every major news source at some point. Given this backdrop, the fact that descriptive language, such as "dependent on government" and "believe that they are victims," is so comfortably presented and utilized by a White politician in front of a primarily White audience is meaningful. This is the language that was used to described African slaves freed after the Civil War and apparently now used to describe a race-less 47% of the public that supports arguably not Obama, but, first and foremost, the Black man occupying the White House! The potency of this attack line only gains credibility and traction to the extent of the continual renewal and regeneration of the racist language and discourse that has been historically utilized. What would Romney's audience make of this "mainstream" critique and the language he used if there had not been a constant production and distribution of overt and subtle racist messages targeted at Obama? What is most striking about the convergence of the fringe and mainstream conservative attacks on Obama is their refusal to disavow and break from past problematic racial discourse. The open and clear use of this racial discourse to engage a potential pool of White voters is unmistakable. It is not simply a matter of a "dog-whistle" show that can cleanly separate the bad fringe-racist part of the conservative movement from the non-racist good part of the mainstream conservative political body. The mutually supporting racial components drive at one goal and rely on the same historical racist discourse. A more persuasive argument could be made for the fact that these comments either led to Romney's downfall or were the final nail in his political coffin, and in that respect, Obama's racial identity became secondary.

What is more peculiar and difficult to assess are the critiques from the left side of the political spectrum. To the extent that critiques that left-based criticisms are based on a more peaceful and egalitarian vision of the world and guided by the principles of a better quality of life for the millions of people that have been neglected, abused, and broken by modern capitalistic society, it is worth assessing how true the Obama administration held to those ideological and political principles. What has been disconcerting has been the way in which critiques from this political bent have been directed specifically at the person in charge of the executive branch, and there has been little discussion about the way in which the executive branch operates and what the implications of having the first African American president might mean for the day-to-day operations of the executive branch.

On one level, critiques from the left leveled at Obama on a personal level are understandable and well documented. In particular, expressing disappointment with Obama because of campaign promises he had not accomplished is a common concern and has been expressed by activists, academics, and the general public. Rarely, though, has been a more thorough and engaging analysis of these promises been done from the standpoint of what past presidents have accomplished and even from the vantage point of what is possible for the executive branch to accomplish within the context of the tripartite form of federal government. Put another way, how many of Obama's promises were realistic goals, not just from the standpoint of what a liberal Democrat should and could advocate for and accomplish, but also from the standpoint of what any president could accomplish within a White Nationalist framework? To examine this question, I would like to turn to the work of Eduardo Bonilla-Silva. In one of the additional chapters in his book, *Racism Without Racists: Color-Blind Racism and Racial Inequality in Contemporary America*, he provides a wide-ranging critique of Obama from the left. His critique is emblematic of many of the scathing attacks Obama has received from leftists of many stripes, and it is worthwhile to dissect many critical components of these critiques from the filter of White Nationalism I have utilized throughout this book. Bonilla-Silva (2010) begins his critical review of the Obama administration with the following statement: "In many ways the entire nation succumbed to Obamania. Thankfully some progressive critics had a shield that protected them from this social current" (p. 16). By establishing this context for critiquing the Obama administration, Bonilla-Silva literally makes the racist attacks on Obama invisible. Obviously many conservatives were not swept up in Obamania. This segment of the population should not be lopped off by critiques from the left, as well as the right, and it is important that these racist attacks and the receptive audience that has continued to be receptive to these attacks needed to be included in any thoughtful and thorough analysis of the Obama administration. To simply suggest that Obama had overwhelming electoral and public support can only lead to a profound misunderstanding of the Obama administration, as well as how race relations operate in society today. Not only did a large segment of the White population vote for Senator McCain in 2008, but over 20 states did, and in some states, such as Alabama, 90% of the White men voted for Senator McCain.

These facts speak to the deep-seated racial animosity that plagued the Obama administration.

Even a narrow reading of Bonilla-Silva's opening comments could be considered just as troubling and incongruent. If Bonilla-Silva's comments were directed only at the left and were intended to be a warning to not be overly enthusiastic or politically blinded by Obama's success, then he undercuts the potency of this argument by claiming: "First, given that this country does not have a traditional left and has extremely weak labor unions (Aronowitz, 1991) it has never been easy to be a progressive in America" (Bonilla-Silva, 2010). Starting with the premise that the left is not large and is politically weak would also seem to imply that the left is largely irrelevant in this country. Where this assessment might not be remarkable or even very controversial, the logical link this statement should have to Obama and other presidents is not just lost on Bonilla-Silva, but so many others that claim to offer leftist critiques of the president. Second, with Obama as president many felt vindicated since many of the concerns, issues, and predictions they made during the campaign became reality. Unfortunately, this vindication was somewhat Pyrrhic as Obama's victory increased madness in the nation and reduced even further the space for criticizing him and his polices from the left (Bonilla-Silva, 2010). What is most striking about these comments is the implied assumption that 1) Obama could ever satisfy what the left in this country claims to want, and 2) that Obama could be so radically different than every other president in history in terms of governing style and public policy advocacy and development. In terms of satisfying the left, Bonilla-Silva smacks right up into this contradiction by stating "All socioeconomic indicators revealed several racial gaps in income, wealth, housing, and educational and occupational standing" (Bonilla-Silva, 2010). If this concerned the leftists that Bonilla-Silva represents, the question that must follow is why would one believe that the president could ever have an impact in these areas? If there has never been a president with this level of racial consciousness and one that has attempted to directly address these racial disparities in a holistic and comprehensive fashion, then what is the logic that leads one to believe that Obama could or should be the first president to do this?

Once again if the dots are connected between Bonilla-Silva's initial insights about the weakness of the left to the dots that suggest that Obama did not do enough in areas such as racial disparity, then the unequivocal final dot must be the sociological insight that people create the conditions under which things can happen. Put another way, how realistic would it be for the president to go against not just where the vast majority of the country is politically, but also against the ideological and political space where the other two branches of government, judicial and congressional, are comfortably situated? It might make sense to hold onto the leftist principles previously articulated, but to suggest that these principles can or should be directed at the president is also a form of madness!

I would also offer that one of the dangers in the type of leftist critique that people like Bonilla-Silva offer is the way in which it can be construed as an argument for permanent failure. The more salient point, given the weak nature of the left that Bonilla-Silva describes, becomes what tangible victories and gains can be made through electoral politics. Bonilla-Silva suggests that "whites ... said without much hesitation that if Obama were like Jesse Jackson or Al Sharpton, they 'probably would like him as much'" (Bonilla-Silva, p. 37, 2010). This is an extremely important insight since Bonilla-Silva is offering this as a critique of how weak and vacuous Obama's racial politics are and how problematic this was for the country. What is fascinating is the fact that Jackson and Sharpton were not the first Black president, and they both lost in the Democratic primaries. Once again, the principle leftist position could extend its logic to only supporting candidates with the level of racial consciousness and commitment of a Sharpton or Jackson and could also ensure that the Democrats would never win a presidential election again! Put bluntly, what comprises are leftists willing to make for electoral gains and incremental changes versus a puritanical approach that would be based on candidates who would never be elected in a national setting. The fact that Obama was the first Black person to ever win a statewide race in Iowa and that this first caucus victory in 2008 catapulted him into the national spotlight as the only "legitimate" Democratic challenger to Senator Hillary Clinton should not be lost in a leftist analysis. It is also worth noting that Reverend Sharpton did not even attempt to campaign in Iowa in 2004. The first two states in the primaries, Iowa and New Hampshire, have very low percentage of non-White residents and voters. By definition, to be a competitive politician in these states one would need to appeal to a White electorate, and tailoring a message for this audience that alienates a vast majority of this audience would be political suicide.

This leftist logic can also be applied to the top three Democratic party candidates for president in 2008, and the question can be asked, "Which of the top three Democrats, Senators Edwards, Clinton, and Obama, was more of a leftist and why?" For example, if one wanted to make the case that Edwards was the most progressive because of his very effective presentation of the "two Americas" and his focus on poverty and class issues, then what would one make of the fact that he ultimately came in third place in the Democratic primaries? Would this mean that there were no gains that someone with a leftist perspective could find in a potential Clinton or Obama presidency? These questions can lead to a type of analysis that can highlight exactly what some of the Obama administration's accomplishments were and an assessment of whether they were and are worthy of leftists' support. These questions could also be applied larger to the political audience of Americans in general and one may ask whether or not any of these accomplishments are noteworthy and/or worthy of support.

ACCOMPLISHMENTS AND FAILURES OF THE OBAMA ADMINISTRATION

A discussion of what the Obama administration was able to achieve and how these achievements have been received provides an excellent starting place for a critical review. The following list from Paul Glastris, Ryan Cooper, and Siyu Hu (2012) describes the top five public policy accomplishments from the Obama administration:

1 Passed Health Care Reform: After five presidents over a century failed to create universal health insurance, signed the Affordable Care Act (2010). It will cover 32 million uninsured Americans beginning in 2014 and mandates a suite of experimental measures to cut health care cost growth, the number one cause of America's long-term fiscal problems.

2 Passed the Stimulus: Signed $787 billion American Recovery and Reinvestment Act in 2009 to spur economic growth amid greatest recession since the Great Depression. Weeks after stimulus went into effect, unemployment claims began to subside. Twelve months later, the private sector began producing more jobs than it was losing, and it has continued to do so for twenty-three straight months, creating a total of nearly 3.7 million new private-sector jobs.

3 Passed Wall Street Reform: Signed the Dodd-Frank Wall Street Reform and Consumer Protection Act (2010) to re-regulate the financial sector after its practices caused the Great Recession. The new law tightens capital requirements on large banks and other financial institutions, requires derivatives to be sold on clearinghouses and exchanges, mandates that large banks provide "living wills" to avoid chaotic bankruptcies, limits their ability to trade with customers' money for their own profit, and creates the Consumer Financial Protection Bureau (now headed by Richard Cordray) to crack down on abusive lending products and companies.

4 Ended the War in Iraq: Ordered all U.S. military forces out of the country. Last troops left on December 18, 2011.

5 Began Drawdown of War in Afghanistan: From a peak of 101,000 troops in June 2011, U.S. forces are now down to 91,000, with 23,000 slated to leave by the end of summer 2012. According to Secretary of Defense Leon Panetta, the combat mission there will be over by next year (p. 1).

This list provides one lens through which the Obama administration can be viewed and evaluated. With the possible exception of health care reform, one could argue that any Democratic president elected in 2008 would have the same legislative agenda and probably the same level of success in these areas. On one level, this argument would also seem to undercut the validity and the significance of the racial attacks on Obama. On another level, it is clear from the racial hyperbole of the fringe end of the conservative movement, as well as the polite racial discourse built in and around the racial hyperbole, a convincing case could be made that conservatives and Republican party supporters were going to utilize a racial discourse to their advantage against any African American candidate representing the Democratic party. If Obama has been able to accomplish as much or more than other liberal-moderate Democratic presidents, then why would the racism directed at him matter? In hindsight one could even argue that this was not only an ineffective and detrimental tactic and strategy to use in the elections of 2008 and 2012, but that overt and subtle racist attacks on Obama continued to not produce tangible and worthwhile political results. In terms of policies that would appear to be progressive or more ideologically left-based, certainly a case could be made for more formidable political resistance coming from the other major political party and from those that espouse conservative political beliefs. Put another way, if Obama really was the boogie Black man caricature that has been created for him, something like the candidacies of Reverends Jackson or Sharpton and the visions of America they offered the electorate, and if Obama was advocating what could be more clearly identified as very ideologically left-based positions and policies, then the level of racial hyperbole coming from pundit sources, such as Coulter and Limbaugh, and from politically rooted sources, such as Romney and McCain, would make a lot more sense. Counter-racial arguments against what are presented as specific race-based policies with the clear intention to help racial minorities could arguably be a much more familiar and common part of past historical racial discourse. What then has been remarkable has not been the lack of accomplishments for Obama, or even an inability to govern effectively; the point would be that he has done all of this while under the most intense racial attacks and scrutiny. Even the most mundane and simple acts of the White House have been ridiculed and challenged. From First Lady Michelle Obama's program to raise awareness about healthy food and encourage exercise for children to President Obama's comments about Trayvon Martin to even the invitation from the White House to the musician Common, all of these actions have met with the most cynical and brutal backlash from many conservative corners. (Linkins, 2011).

Highlighting these accomplishments, it is possible to glean a narrative of a successful moderate or liberal presidency for Obama and that this success would seem to defy the potency and the force of the racist attacks that have been leveled at Obama. It would be a much more difficult argument to articulate to suggest how much more Obama would be able to have accomplished if he was not "tarred and feathered" with racial attacks. The more coherent and clearly identifiable argument that can be made is the one that Walters expresses. When moved to the realm of specific policy examples to measure the Obama presidency that directly impact the most disadvantaged racial minorities in our society, one can begin to understand the relevancy and stubborn persistence of policy racism and party convergence. Walters' laser-like focus on anti-poverty programs, education, and the criminal justice system can be understood as most revealing not just from the standpoint of where the least amount of change in public policy and conditions on the ground have occurred but from the vantage point of how little any political party or individual has been able to produce substantial change in the last 40 years.

This can be seen in the most sympathetic reading of some of Obama's most progressive policy initiatives and success. Whether one would want to include Attorney General Holder's vociferous support of the Voting Rights Act, Obama's willingness to not defend the Defense of Marriage Act and his support for marriage equality, Obama's policy directive to make a certain population of children of undocumented families safe from deportation and eligible for work visas, the nomination and support of the first Latina for the Supreme Court (Supreme Court Justice Sotomayor), support for congressional Democrats' effort to end the Bush tax cuts for the wealthiest portion of American families, or even the first legislative act he signed (the Lilly Ledbetter Fair Pay Act) that provided women and racial minorities greater protection from workplace discrimination by changing the statute of limitations for equal-pay worker claims, all of these accomplishments could be scrutinized from the vantage point of the destitute existence that many racial minorities struggle with on a daily basis and the potential connection these social conditions can have to government policies and programs. The fundamental question revolves around to what extent these accomplishments or any other accomplishments actually scratch the surface of the profound and horrific conditions millions of racial minorities struggle with every day.

Another way to appreciate how steep a political climb it might be for a president to adequately address this racial quandary can be seen in the added element of the financial collapse of 2008. George Condon, Jr. and Jim O'Sullivan provide an insightful glimpse into many of the twists and turns for this racial and political conundrum in their article. Condon and O'Sullivan (2013) ground their work in the daily life experiences of many African Americans: "The Great Recession may be over for the country as a whole, but they aren't feeling the recovery" (p. 1). Condon and Sullivan present the Great Recession in explicit racial terms for the African American community: "Black unemployment remains double that for whites," and "The median income gap between white and black households has hit a record high. Blacks have half the access to health care as whites" (p. 1). Condon and O'Sullivan boldly conclude with this insight: "The gap in homeownership is wider today than it was in 1990. African Americans are twice as likely as whites to have suffered foreclosure" (p. 1). One statistic Condon and O'Sullivan (2013) utilize illustrates perfectly the degree to which the economic collapse of 2008 has wreaked havoc on African Americans: "Net wealth for black families dropped by 27.1 percent during the recession" (p. 1). This insight, coupled with the information of epidemic proportions of African Americans in the criminal justice system provided by Condon and O'Sullivan, illustrates how dire and entrenched these social, economic, and political problems have become for many African Americans: "One in 15 African-American men is incarcerated, compared with one in 106 white men. Blacks make up 38 percent of inmates in state and federal prisons. Although only 13.8 percent of the U.S. population, African Americans represent 27 percent of those living below the poverty line" (p. 1).

These statistics present a very bleak picture for millions of African Americans. Their lives seem removed and completely disconnected from so many of the most progressive and successful accomplishments of the Obama administration. Walters' work continues to ring true in terms of the need for federal government policies and programs that can assist the most vulnerable racial minority communities. His specific description and analysis of the executive office's lack of interest and political will, across party lines, in addressing the concerns of these populations can also be applied to the Obama administration. Condon and O'Sullivan carefully detail the way in which key figures in the Obama administration demonstrate their knowledge of these specific issues, as well as how they articulate the administration's response to the deepening crisis of poverty and unemployment for racial minorities since the economic collapse of 2008. One of the sources used in their article is Valerie Jarrett, and she has been described as the most significant African American in the Obama inner circle.

Jarrett's insights provide a glimpse into how Obama might understand and process these issues, and Condon and O'Sullivan (2013) describe her thoughts in the following way:

> Those expectations include programs that can lift urban areas out of poverty, improve inner-city schools, reform the criminal-justice system, and alleviate sky-high black unemployment. All these numbers, Jarrett acknowledges, have been stubbornly resistant to fixes from Washington, none more so than the jobless figures. African Americans are the only demographic group with higher unemployment today than when Obama took office. White unemployment dropped from 7.1 percent in January 2009 to 6.8 percent in February 2013. Hispanic unemployment dropped

from 10.0 percent to 9.6 percent. But African-American unemployment rose from 12.7 percent to 13.8 percent during that time (p. 3).

This passage suggests that Jarrett and the administration were aware of these numbers and that they were actively trying to address these problems. The key point becomes the acknowledgement of Jarrett that these social and economic problems have been "stubbornly resistant to fixes from Washington." On the one hand, this appears to be complete capitulation from the Obama administration with regards to a sincere effort to address these issues, while on the other hand, it could also suggest that even the most aggressive attempt by the executive branch might not make a significant difference in being able to address these types of issues.

An example of how this conundrum can be understood is from the standpoint of the comments offered by a White House official. Condon and O'Sullivan present these remarks in the following way: "A White House official, who asked not to be named, calls those numbers 'unacceptably high' but insists that 'we have made real progress,' with black joblessness on a decline from 16.8 percent in August 2011" (p. 2). Condon and O'Sullivan then add the following statement from this White House official: "We have seen it come down pretty dramatically over the last couple years, and that is not an accident," and "that is the explicit result of administration policies" (p. 2). This unnamed source makes the profound claim that Black joblessness has been on the decline and that this decrease in the unemployment rate is directly linked to administration policy. This begs the question of it being so easy for the administration to successfully intervene and have a positive impact on the unemployment rate for African Americans, then why was it not done earlier and why has this drop in employment been so slow? One could also ask why Obama does not talk about this work and his success in this area, especially if this work is being presented as independent of congressional action and did not require a specific vote to authorize additional funds for any government programs or agencies.

This tension in the official and unofficial statement from Jarrett and the White House staff members does not become any clearer or more coherent when it is also what Condon and O'Sullivan present as being based on the following mantra:

> "Jobs, jobs, jobs has been the central focus of the president's administration since day one," Jarrett said, and also, she noted, at the heart of the "Ladder of Opportunity" program the president laid out in his State of the Union in February and his follow-up speech in Chicago. In his second term, the president is determined to target the most stubborn pockets of unemployment in urban areas, another White House aide said, pointing out that a part of the American Jobs Act—which remains untouched by Congress—"would provide subsidized employment for the long-term unemployed in this country, which would disproportionately benefit many people of color" (p. 1).

This passage then moves theses social and economic issues into the more familiar terrain of the quagmire of Washington, DC, politics and the reality of split-party control of the House and the Senate. Once Obama's initiatives are linked to specific legislation, such as the American Jobs Act, that will remain permanently stuck in Congress and will never see the light of day as long as the House of Representatives is controlled by the Republican party, then the argument can be succinctly made by the Obama administration that their hands are tied. They cannot successfully address issues, such as the dire social and economic conditions with which millions of racial minorities struggle, as long as one part of Congress, the House of Representatives, is controlled by an opposing political party that is unwilling to consider any legislative initiatives from the president or any elected Democratic officials in the House or the Senate. This point also fundamentally contradicts the earlier insight from an unnamed White

House official that suggested the Obama administration was directly responsible for the unemployment rate for African Americans dropping below 16%.

The tension between what impact the executive branch can have on providing assistance to the most vulnerable communities of color and an administration that publicly advocates for "race-less" policies is exacerbated by the historical legacy of racism in the executive branch, as well as the specific racism that has been directed at Obama. Condon and O'Sullivan suggest that this dynamic is most pronounced when Jarrett describes the legislative success of this "race-less" approach by the administration with the passage of the Patient Protection and Affordable Care Act: "Health care reform is at the top of that list." Condon and O'Sullivan then place this within the appropriate context Jarrett lays out, "'Approximately 7 million African Americans are without health insurance,' Jarrett said" (p. 3). From this vantage point it is easy to present the racial implications and significance of Obama's work, as well as highlight his "post-racial" mission, as stated by Jarret within the context of Condon and O'Sullivan's work: "'So, yes, it is a policy that disproportionately does benefit the African-American community. But it also disproportionately benefits poor people'" (p. 1). What is most striking about this example is not how well this internal logic of a "race-less" policy can be used to explain and support a policy that has a disproportionate positive impact on African Americans most in need of support, but the unacknowledged grueling history that brought this legislation to life. A prime example given earlier of the way in which the racial attacks that were unleashed against Obama's "race-less" policies was health care legislation. Conservative pundits, such as Rush Limbaugh, presented Obamacare as reparations for African Americans. Besides all of the typical and untraditional tactics and strategies used to oppose this legislation both before and after it become law, conservative pundits also attempted to "racialize" this issue. The suggestion that health care would only benefit African Americans and that Obama was pursing this policy as support for his "racial" group was not accidental or a subtle reframing of the national debate. It fit into the larger overt and subtle racial attacks that had started with the launch of his presidential campaign. Jarrett's discussion does not include this critical point. Given the fact that this legislation barely passed with a Democratic majority in the House and the Senate, had to survive legal challenges up to the Supreme Court level, and to this day is actively being challenged by the Republican party through tactics and strategies that included shutting down the entire federal government, it is safe to say that these "raceless" policies are not very easy to advocate for and accomplish. It is possible to even ask if specific race-based policies would have an easier or more difficult time surviving in this realm of federal politics. This brings the discussion back to the fundamental point about Obama's racial identity and the overt and subtle racial attacks this identity has elicited. It has played a critical role in blocking his legislative agenda, and it has played a significant role in how he has developed and advocated for public policies.

One can see that based on this listing of the successes, as well as the shortcomings, of the Obama administration and the analysis of these areas offered by White House officials, that Walters' notion of White Nationalism also anticipated all of these challenges for the executive branch and for the specific challenges that the first African American president might encounter. As part of Walters' argument for the existence and maintenance of White Nationalism within the executive branch, a direct connection is evident between the lack of adequate support from the federal government for the most vulnerable communities of color and the way both Democratic and Republican presidential administrations have reinforced and nurtured these racial dynamics. Whether through overt support of racist policies or the lack of political will and interest to challenge these policies, affirmative action, anti-poverty programs, and the criminal justice system represented the most noticeable and blatant areas of racism with the executive branch, according to Walters. Walters' text then provides a model of how to understand and explain the growth of and the intensity of attacks on President Obama and his administration and why these attacks are so integral to the racial discourse. The type of federal government that has historically had the greatest impact on transforming African American lives (Reconstruction Period and Civil Rights Era) provides the basis for his analysis and the rationale for why these types of race-targeted programs are still needed and why they would also be extremely difficult for even the most progressive executive branch to successfully advocate for and support. Jarrett's presentation of the most significant legislative success for the Obama administration in terms of the "raceless" approach is revealing in the way that all "race" roads seem to lead to one inevitable, gloomy conclusion for the actual possibility of the federal government being able to play any positive substantial role in the lives of millions of people of color.

The epigraph at the beginning of this work is based on an all-too-familiar story, as presented by Earnest McBride, of an African American man who seemed to deviate from acceptable etiquette and decorum and was properly disciplined to put him back on course. Whether from the standpoint of a DuBoisian notion of a double consciousness or from the simple stories relived every day by racial minorities, the basic premise of trying to fulfill the established norms and customs of the dominant White society while at the same time staying true to one's authentic "other" self is a dilemma deeply embedded in American consciousness. When Dr. J.A. Miller attempted to express his constitutionally protected right to free speech, he was brutally punished and shamed. Expressing disapproval of selling war bonds was not just a public policy debate or intellectual curiosity, but it was part of a murky, dangerous racial terrain. In stepping into this void, Miller made not just the case for why it might be reasonable to not want to sell war bonds for World War I, but he also decisively stepped into the racial terrain of defiance and disrespect. McBride (2009) goes on to describe how this could not be tolerated, and the tarring-and-feathering punishment seemed to fit the nature of the crime:

> Because of this public statement, racist mayor J.J. Hayes instigated the mob action that led to the tarring and feathering of Dr. Miller before he was ridden around downtown Vicksburg on a rail and forced to stand in front of City Hall for nearly half a day wearing a sign saying "I am disloyal to the United States Government." The good doctor was then put on a

train and told by the mayor and the police chief never
to return to Mississippi on pain of losing his life (p. 7).

It is within this same racial preoccupation and obsession that we find the
context for the Obama presidency. Each action, each thought presented
and dissected by Obama was filtered through this racial logic, and there
is still a large and receptive audience for these racial dynamics. It is not
then a matter of Obama being rendered powerless and incapable of any
decision. Just as Dr. Miller was well within his right to decide to sell war
bonds and "go along with" the project, Obama had to be acutely aware
of the fact that he was confronted with the same personal dilemma. Policy
decisions and executive actions that deviate from previously established
norms risk being scrutinized in a racial-reactionary fashion. This could
be seen most clearly in the debate around health care reform and the
inflammatory comments about African American reparations that were
used in some of the critiques of the Obama-supported health care reform legislation. The same could be said about policies, decisions, and
executive actions that represent continuity and consistency from the
previous administrations. This can especially be seen in foreign-policy
areas, such as the use of drones and the inability to close Guantanamo
Bay, where many expected that Obama would significantly move away
from the foreign-policy and executive-branch decisions associated with
the previous Bush administration. In the process of recognizing and
acknowledging how these dynamics factor into how Obama was able to
gain power and how he governed, a more useful and valuable assessment
of his presidency can be conducted. To not incorporate these dynamics
into the analysis would run the risk of suggesting that race doesn't matter
and that Obama's was a "raceless" presidency. It would also make the
dual burden non-White politicians face on a regular basis invisible and
potentially make it even more difficult for non-White politicians to enter
and engage in traditional political spheres and institutions. To not include
an analysis of race in the way Feagin, Omi, Winant, and Weber have
described and connect this analysis to a specific examination of the way
Walters describes how White Nationalism operates on the executive level

risks being incomplete and inaccurate. Through their work it is possible to ascertain how not just Obama's personal racial identity has been a target for attack, but also how these attacks are connected to the way institutional and systemic racism operate in society. From this vantage point Obama's "tarred-and-feathered" moments can be more clearly identified and ana-lyzed. The previous discussion about his defense of Gates and critique of the Cambridge incident can be seen as a similar Dr. Miller moment and a similar "mob punishment" for this breach of racial decorum. It is also within this space that a broader discussion about what risks and courage Obama should have and could have mustered on a daily basis could be weighed on a scale with the political backlash he might have encountered. This equation is quite often misunderstood and/or neglected with minori-ty politicians, and these dynamics are most pronounced on the level of the presidency. This racial impact will have a lingering effect on not just executive-branch-level politics but also on day-to-day race relations, long after Obama's two terms as president.

REFERENCES

American Library Association, "Shirley Chisholm—Her historic run for Congress and president influenced generations," http://dev.atyourlibrary.org/culture/shirley-chisholm-her-historic-run-congress-and-president-influenced-generations

Associated Press. (2004, Jan. 15). "Moseley Braun ends campaign, endorses Dean." NBC News. Retrieved from http://www.nbcnews.com/id/3962175/

Bailey, P. (2007, Oct. 29). "From bible belt to Nobel Prize," *St. Petersburg Times.*

Balz, D. (2007, Feb. 1). "Biden stumbles at the starting gate comments about Obama overtake bid for president," *Washington Post.*

Barker, L. J. (1989). "Jesse Jackson's candidacy in political-social perspective: A contextual analysis." *Jesse Jackson's 1984 Presidential Campaign: Challenge and Change in American Politics,* L.J. Barker and R.W. Walters (Eds.). Urbana, IL: University of Illinois Press.

Bell, D. (2008). *Race, racism, and American law,* Sixth Edition. New York, NY: Wolters Kluwer Law and Business.

Bjerga, Alan and Oldham, Jennifer. (2012, January 20). "Gingrich Calling Obama 'Food-Stamp President' Draws Critics." *Bloomberg.*

Bonilla-Silva, E. (2010) *Racism without racists: Color-blind racism and the persistence of racial inequality in America,* Oxford, UK: Rowman and Littlefield Publishers, Inc.

Buell, Jr., E. & Sigelman, L. (2008) *Attack politics: Negativity in presidential campaigns since 1960,* Lawrence, KS: University Press of Kansas.

Bunch, S. (2012, June 12) "Healthcare reform isn't 'reparations,'" Bunch Blog. Retrieved from http://sonnybunch.com/healthcare-reform-isnt-reparations/

Carpenter, Tim, (2009, August 26), "Jenkins' remark raises eyebrows," The Topeka Capital-Journal cjonline.com. Retrieved from http://cjonline.com/news-state/2009-08-26/jenkins-remark-raises-eyebrows

Clarkson, F. (2008, March 27). "Wright wrongly receives far more coverage than Coe, Hagee and Parsley," *Talk to Action.* Retrieved from http://www.talk2action.org/story/2008/3/27/13119/4751

Condon, Jr., G.E. & O'Sullivan, J. (2013, Apr. 5). "Has President Obama done enough for black Americans?" *The Atlantic.*

democracy8888, (2008, Jan. 13), "Dick Gregory's '68 run for the White House," *Daily Kos.*

Dowd, Maureen, (2009, Sep. 12). "Boy, Oh, Boy," *New York Times.*

Duclos, S. (2008, May 14). "Controversy created by tavern selling Obama 'Curious George' t-shirts." *Digital Journal.*

Dyson, Michael Eric. (2015, April 15). "The Ghost of Cornel West What happened to America's most exciting black scholar?" *The New Republic.*

Ellis, R. & Dedrick, M. (1997). "The Presidential candidate, then and now." *Perspectives on Political Science, 26.*

Feagin, J. (2001). *Racist America: Roots, current realties, and future reparations,* Second Edition. New York, NY: Routledge.

Finkelstein, M. (2007, October 20). "Obama: No hand on heart for National Anthem," *NewsBusters.* Retrieved from http://newsbusters.org/blogs/mark-finkelstein/2007/10/20/obama-no-hand-heart-pledge-either-will-msm-notice

Fishman, D. (2013). "Racial attacks on President Obama and the White Nationalist legacy," *The Western Journal of Black Studies, 37*(4), 236–248.

Freeman, J. (2005, Feb.). "Shirley Chisholm's 1972 presidential campaign," JoFreeman.com.

Frick, A. (2008, Sep. 13). "'Obama waffles' featuring racist, stereotyped images sold at values voter summit," *Think Progress.* Retrieved from http://think-progress.org/2008/09/13/obama-waffles-featuring-racist-stereotyped-images-sold-at-values-voter-summit/

Fusco, C. & Pallasch, A.M. (2008, Apr. 18). "Who is Bill Ayers?" *Chicago Sun Times.*

Gandy, K., (2005, Jan. 3). "NOW honors guts and glory of Shirley Chisholm," National Organization of Women. Retrieved from http://www.elegantbrain.com/academic/department/AandL/AAS/ANNOUNCE/shirleychisholm/now.html

Genovese, M. (2001). *The power of the American presidency: 1789–2000.* New York, NY: Oxford University Press, Inc.

Glastris, P., Cooper, R., & Hu, S., (2012, Mar./Apr.). "Obama's top 50 accomplishments," *Washington Monthly.*

Habeeb, Lee. (2013, July 23). "A White Person's Reaction to Obama's Trayvon Martin Speech," *National Review.* Retrieved from http://www.nationalreview.com/article/354209/white-persons-reaction-obamas-trayvon-martin-speech-lee-habeeb

Hansen, S. (2002, Feb. 20). "Why blacks love Bill Clinton," *Salon.* http://www.salon.com/2002/02/21/clinton_88/

Heilemann, J. & Halperin, M. (2010). *Game change: Obama and the Clintons, McCain and Palin, and the race of a lifetime.* New York, NY: Harper Collins Publishers.

Hennessey, K. & Memoli, M. A. (2010, July 12). "NAACP set to denounce tea party for racism," *Los Angeles Times.*

Hill, J. B. (2009). *The first black president: Barack Obama, race, politics, and the American dream.* New York, NY: Palgrave McMillan.

Hooper, M. K. (2009, Sept. 9). "'You lie': Rep. Wilson apologizes for yell," *The Hill.*

Hoppe, C. (2008, June 19). "Vendor who sold racist Obama pin apologizes," *The Dallas Morning News.*

Hulse, C. (2008, February 28). "McCain's canal zone birth prompts queries about whether that rules him out," *New York Times.*

Hutchinson, E. O. (2009, August 13). "Method to racist madness in fresh racial attacks on President Obama" *Huffington Post*. Retrieved from http://www. huffingtonpost.com/earl-ofari-hutchinson/method-to-racist-madness-_b_3749451.html

Johnston, Lauren (2004, Jan 15). "Braun Quits Race, Backs Dean," CBS/AP. Retrieved from https://www.cbsnews.com/news/braun-quits-race-backs-dean/

Juliano, N. (2008, Feb. 25). "Obama camp blasts Clinton for 'Obama in Muslim garb' photo," *therawstory*. Retrieved from http://rawstory.com/news/2008/Obama_campaign_blasts_Clinton_over_photo_0225.html

Kalven, J. (2006, Dec.). "Schlussel: Should Barack Hussein Obama be president when we are fighting the war of our lives against Islam?" *MediaMatters for America*, Retrieved from http://mediamatters.org/research/200612200005

Kelly, D. (2008, Oct. 17). "Newsletter's Obama illustration denounced: Leader of GOP club denies racist intent in use of stereotypes," *Los Angeles Times*.

Klein, E. (2010, Feb. 22). "Rush Limbaugh: Health-care reform is 'reparations,' a 'civil rights act.'" *Washington Post*. Retrieved from http://voices.washington-post.com/ezra-klein/2010/02/rush_limbaugh_health-care_refo.html

Kornreich, Lauren, (2009, Aug. 28). "Congresswoman apologizes for 'great white hope' comment." *CNN*.

Levingston, S. E. (2010, April 30). "Reagan and the occult," *Washington Post*.

Linkins, J. (2011, May 10) "Outrage flares as Michelle Obama invites Common to White House to read poetry," *Huffington Post*.

Llamas, T. (2004, March 5). "Tommy Llamas on Al Sharpton, the campaign embeds." MSNBC. http://www.nbcnews.com/id/3087356/

Love, D. A. (2013, October 21). "The Willie Horton ad revisited 25 years later." *The Grio*. http://thegrio.com/2013/10/21/the-willie-horton-ad-revisited-25-years-later/

Malcolm, A. (2008, April 17). "Barack Obama removes his U.S. flag lapel pin once more," *Los Angeles Times*.

Manring, M.M. (1998). *Slave in a Box: The strange career of Aunt Jemima.* Charlottesville, VA: The University Press of Virginia.

Maraniss, D. (2012). *Barack Obama: The story.* New York, NY: Simon and Schuster Paperbacks.

Martin, R. (2008, March 21). "The full story behind Wright's 'God damn America' sermon." CNN. Retrieved from http://ac360.blogs.cnn.com/2008/03/21/the-full-story-behind-wright%E2%80%99s-%E2%80%9Cgod-damn-ameri-ca%E2%80%9D-sermon/

McBride, E. (2009, Mar. 26–Apr. 1). "1918–1919: White terrorists tar and feather black women in Vicksburg," *Jackson Advocate*.

Merrill, L., Nanez, D., & Bennett, L. (2013, Aug. 8). "Hundreds protest Obama outside Phoenix high school." *The Republic*.

Morris, L. & Williams, L. F. (1989). "The coalition at the end of the rainbow: The 1984 Jackson campaign." *Jesse Jackson's 1984 Presidential Campaign: Challenge and Change in American Politics*. L.J. Barker and R. W. Walters (Eds.). Urbana, Illinois: University of Illinois Press.

Nordin, D. S. (2012) *From Edward Brooke to Barack Obama: African American political success, 1966–2008*. Columbia, MO: University of Missouri Press.

Obama, B. (2008). *The audacity of hope: Thoughts on reclaiming the American dream*. New York, NY: Vintage Books.

Obama, B. (2007). *Dreams from my father: A story of race and inheritance*. New York, NY: Random House, Inc.

Obama, B. (2004, July 27) "Transcript: Illinois Senate Candidate Barack Obama," *Washington Post*. Retrieved from http://www.washingtonpost.com/wp-dyn/articles/A19751-2004Jul27.html.

Ogletree, C. (2010). *The presumption of guilt: The arrest of Henry Louis Gates, Jr. and race, class and crime in America*. New York, NY: Palgrave-Macmillan.

Omi, M. & Winant, H. (1996). *Racial formation in the United States: From the 1960s to the 1980s*, New York, NY: Routledge.

Page, C. (2004, Feb. 11) "What a friend Bush has in the Rev. Al Sharpton," *Chicago Tribune*. Retrieved from http://articles.chicagotribune.com/2004-02-11/news/0402110264_1_rev-al-sharpton-black-districts-black-voters.

Palast, G., (2004, June 21). "Baby Bush and the Florida and Ohio vote," *Common Dreams*. Retrieved from http://www.commondreams.org/views04/0621-11.htm.

Pfifner, J. P. (2011). *The Modern Presidency*. Sixth Edition. Boston, MA: Wadsworth.

Purnick, J. & Oreskes, M. (1987, Nov. 29). "Jesse Jackson aims for the mainstream." *The New York Times*.

Rolph, A. (2008, Aug. 27) "Snohomish County GOP apologizes for fake Obama bills," *Seattle Times*.

Rosenberg, P. (2008, Aug. 2). "Colorblind racism and the conservative racist attacks on Obama, Sotomayor as 'racist.'" *Open Left*. Retrieved from http://openleft.com/diary/14460/colorblind-racism-the-conservative-racist-attacks-on-obama-sotomayor-as-racist.

Ross, B. & El-Buri, R. (2008, Mar. 13). "Obama's pastor: God damn America, U.S. to blame for 9/11," ABC News. Retrieved from http://abcnews.go.com/Blotter/DemocraticDebate/story?id=4443788&page=1

Scheff, L. (2003, Apr. 22), "Stealing the 2000 presidential election: Racism, theft, and fraud in Florida," *The Weekly Dig*.

Seelye, K. Q. (2008, May 6) "Wright dominated news coverage," *New York Times*.

Shane, S. (2008, Oct. 3). "Obama and '60s bomber: A look into crossed paths." *New York Times*.

Sheppard, K. (2008, Aug. 23) "Green party presidential candidate Cynthia McKinney talks to Grist." *Grist*. Retrieved from http://grist.org/article/mckinney/.

Sklar, Rachel. (2008, Jul. 21), "Yikes! Controversial New Yorker Cover Shows Muslim, Flag-Burning, Osama-Loving, Fist-Bumping Obama," *Huffington Post*.

Smith, B. (2008, Feb. 22). "Obama once visited '60s radicals," POLITICO. Retrieved from http://www.politico.com/news/stories/0208/8630.html.

Sullivan, A. (2012, Jan. 16). "How Obama's long game will outsmart his critics," *Newsweek*.

Sweet, L. (2008, Feb. 26). "Clothes make the controversy," *Chicago Sun-Times.* Retrieved from http://www.suntimes.com/news/sweet/812719,CST-NWS-sweet26.article.

Tapper, J. & Venkataraman, N. (2007, Jan. 24). "Obama goes on campaign to debunk Madrassa education allegation," ABC News. Retrieved from http://abcnews.go.com/Politics/story?id=2819634&page=1.

Thornburgh, N. (2008, Feb. 28). "Why is Obama's middle name taboo?" *Time.*

Thornton Dill, B. (Ed.). (2009). *Emerging intersections: Race, class, and gender in theory, policy, and practice.* Newark, NJ: Rutgers University Press.

Tulis, J. (1987). *The rhetorical presidency.* Princeton, NJ: Princeton University Press.

Vamburkar, M. (2012, Nov. 5). "Ann Coulter to Hannity: Americans afraid to vote against Obama because 'they'll be accused of racism.'" *MEDIAite.*

Walters, R. (1988). *Black presidential politics in America: A strategic approach.* Albany, NY: State University of New York Press.

Walters, R. (1999) "The emergent mobilization of the black community in the Jackson campaign for president," *Jesse Jackson's 1984 Presidential Campaign: Challenge and Change in American Politics.* L.J. Barker & R.W. Walters (Eds.). Urbana, Illinois: University of Illinois Press.

Waters, R. (2009, Winter). "Former Democratic Congresswoman Cynthia McKinney flirts with Holocaust deniers," *Intelligence Report, 136,* Southern Poverty Law Center. http://www.splcenter.org/get-informed/intelligence-report/browse-all-issues/2009/winter/crossing-the-line.

Walters, R. (2007). *Freedom is not enough: Black voters, black candidates, and American presidential politics.* Lanham, MD: Rowman & Littlefield Publishers.

Walters, R. (1995). *Pan Africanism in the African diaspora: An analysis of modern Afrocentric political movements.* Detroit, MI: Wayne State University Press.

Walters, R. (2008). *The price of racial reconciliation.* Ann Arbor, MI: University of Michigan Press.

Walters, R. (2003). *White Nationalism, black interests: Conservative public policy and the black community.* Detroit, MI: Wayne State University Press.

Walters, R. and Smith, R.C. (1999). *African American leadership.* Albany, NY: State University of New York Press.

Weber, L. (2001). *Understanding race, class, gender, and sexuality: A conceptual framework,* New York, NY: McGraw-Hill Higher Education.

Whitaker, M.C. (2013, Aug. 8). "Racist taunts at Obama should worry us all." CNN. http://www.cnn.com/2013/08/08/opinion/whitaker-obama-arizona-race/index.html.

Williams, P. (1992). *The alchemy of race and rights.* Boston, MA: Harvard University Press.

Wise, T. (2009). *Between Barack and a hard place: Racism and white denial in the age of Obama.* San Francisco, CA: City Lights Books.

Wright, D. & Miller, S. (2007, Oct. 4). "Obama dropped flag pin in war statement." ABC News. http://abcnews.go.com/Politics/ story?id=3690000&page=1

Zeleny, J. (2010, Jan. 9). "Reid apologizes for remarks on Obama's color and 'dialect.'" *New York Times.*

INTERNET WEB SITES AND VIDEO CLIPS

- Information about the Birthers and the Birther Movement:
    - http://www.birthers.org/
    - http://gawker.com/5320465/the-birthers-who-are-they-and-what-do-they-want
- Information about President Obama's birth certificate:
    - http://www.factcheck.org/elections-2008/born_in_the_usa.html
- Senator Richard Shelby's comments on President's Obama's birth certificate:
    - http://www.huffingtonpost.com/2009/02/22/richard-shel-by-alabamase_n_168913.html
- Cokie Roberts comments about the Obamas vacationing in Hawaii:
    - http://www.talkingpointsmemo.com/archives/207883.php
- The actual Fox News clip included in coverage by CNN as a web link:
    - http://www.cnn.com/2007/POLITICS/01/22/obama.madrassa/
- Actual video clip of Steve Doocy's comments on Youtube:
    - http://www.youtube.com/watch?v=nw6LBbeXTww
- Bill Ayers and the Weather Underground controversy:
    - http://en.wikipedia.org/wiki/Bill_Ayers_presidential_election_controversy

- The Future of Freedom:
    - http://www.fff.org/freedom/0400f.asp
- Anti-Defamation League:
    - http://www.adl.org/main_Anti_Semitism_Domestic/default.htm
- Reverend Jeremiah Wright's controversial sermon on YouTube:
    - http://www.youtube.com/watch?v=nH5ixmT83JE
- Comparison of candidates Obama and McCain web pages:
    - http://www.obama-mccain.info/compare-obama-mccain-national-security.php
- FAIR (Fairness and Accuracy In Reporting):
    - "Obama's 'Missing' Flag Pin Trivia Again Distracts Media From Issues Voters Care About," October 10, 2007.
- *Huffington Post*, "10 Most Offensive Tea Party Signs and Extensive Photo Coverage From Tax Day Protests (PHOTOS)," April 16, 2009. Retrieved from http://www.huffingtonpost.com/2009/04/16/10-most-offensive-tea-par_n_187554.html
- History on the Net, "The Coon Caricature: Blacks as monkeys," (Last modified July, 2012), https://www.historyonthenet.com/authentichistory/diversity/african/3-coon/6-monkey/
- Diversity Inc., "New Data on Tea Party & Racism," April 12, 2010. Retrieved from http://www.diversityinc.com/content/1757/article/7481/
- Institute for Research & Education on Human Rights (IREHR), "The Tea Party Movement in 2015," October 2010. (The report was prepared for the NAACP's 106th national convention in Philadelphia, Pennsylvania.) Retrieved from https://www.irehr.org/2015/09/15/the-tea-party-movement-in-2015/
- CBS News, "Mayor Hits Rough Patch Over Watermelon Pic," February 25, 2009. Retrieved from http://www.cbsnews.com/stories/2009/02/25/national/main4827964.shtml

- MediaMatters for America, "Tucker Carlson on Obama's Church: "[I]t's Hard to Call that Christianity," February 9, 2007. Retrieved from http://mediamatters.org/research/200702090009

- MediaMatters for America, "Fox News' E.D. Hill Teased Discussion of Obama Dap: "A Fist Bump? A pPound? A Terrorist Fist Jab?" June 6, 2008. Retrieved from http://mediamatters.org/mmtv/200806060007

- ThinkProgress, January 19, 2007, "Obama Smeared As Former 'Madrassa' Student, Possible Covert Muslim Extremist."

- CNN, October 5th ,2012, TRANSCRIPTS. Retrieved from http://www.cnn.com/TRANSCRIPTS/1210/05/es.01.html

- YouTube, "Fist Pound—Terrorist Fist Jab?" July, 2008. Retrieved from http://www.youtube.com/watch?v=cQfbbSQ5FXY

- Three of the Most Racist Anti-Obama Political Attacks
    - By Nadra Kareem Nittle, About.com Guide

      Updated June 28, 2011.

      http://racerelations.about.com/od/trailblazers/a/Three-Of-The-Most-Racist-Anti-Obama-Political-Attacks_2.htm

- Racist Ole Miss Students Riot Over Obama Win
    - 11/7/2012 6:56 pm by John Aravosis 63 Comments

      AMERICAblog News

      HuffPost Earl Ofari Hutchinson.

- Method to Racist Madness in Fresh Racial Attacks on President Obama
    - Posted: 08/13/2013 3:09 pm by Earl Ofari Hutchinson, HuffPost

    - http://www.huffingtonpost.com/earl-ofari-hutchinson/method-to-racist-madness-_b_3749451.html

- The 10 Worst Moments of Disrespect Towards President Obama
    - January 27, 2012 by Lauren Victoria Burke, politic365.com

- http://politic365.com/2012/01/27/the-10-worst-moments-of-disrespect-towards-president-obama/

- Racial Slurs at College Protests Prompt a Deeper Look Yamiche Alcindor, *USA Today*, November 12, 2012

- The Jed Report from *The Daily Kos*, July 29, 2013.

- Transcript: Obama's News Conference, CBS News, July 23, 2009. Retrieved from https://www.cbsnews.com/news/transcript-obamas-news-conference/

- Remarks by the President on Trayvon Martin, The White House, Office of the Press Secretary, July 19, 2013. Retrieved from https://obamawhitehouse.archives.gov/the-press-office/2013/07/19/remarks-president-trayvon-martin

- The White House, My Brother's Keeper, February 2014. Retrieved from: https://obamawhitehouse.archives.gov/node/279811

- "Mitt Romney on His 47 Percent Comment: 'Actually, I didn't say that.'" http://www.usatoday.com/story/news/2012/11/10/racial-slurs-at-colleges-show-progress-still-needed/1696475/

- Bloomberg

  - "Ole Miss Burnishes Image as Obama Debate Trumps Riot" (Update 1), by Oliver Staley, Sept. 19, 2008. http://www.bloomberg.com/apps/news?pid=newsarchive&sid=amP_M.VdNjE0

CPSIA information can be obtained
at www.ICGtesting.com
Printed in the USA
LVHW01s0417170418
573684LV00004B/6/P

9 781516 529063